FIX-IT and FORGET-IT®
HOLIDAY
INSTANT POT®
COOKBOOK

FIX-IT and FORGET-IT®
HOLIDAY
INSTANT POT®
COOKBOOK

100
Festive and Delicious Favorites

HOPE COMERFORD

Good Books

New York, New York

Good Books books may be purchased in bulk at special discounts for sales promotion, corporate gifts, fund-raising, or educational purposes. Special editions can also be created to specifications. For details, contact the Special Sales Department, Good Books, 307 West 36th Street, 11th Floor, New York, NY 10018 or info@skyhorsepublishing.com.

Good Books is an imprint of Skyhorse Publishing, Inc.®, a Delaware corporation.

Visit our website at www.goodbooks.com.

10 9 8 7 6 5 4 3 2 1

Library of Congress Cataloging-in-Publication Data is available on file.

Cover design by David Ter-Avanesyan
Cover photos by Bonnie Matthews

Print ISBN: 978-1-68099-816-0
Ebook ISBN: 978-1-68099-847-4

Printed in China

Contents

Welcome to Fix-It and Forget-It Holiday Instant Pot Cookbook

In my family, like so many other families around the world, the holidays bring us together with those we care most about. And what better way to celebrate with those we love than with the foods we love?

I asked our Fix-It and Forget-It community to tell me what their favorite holiday dishes were, and they did not disappoint! I have compiled 100 incredibly delicious recipes that will satisfy your holiday cravings and traditions. All the recipes in this book are designed for the Instant Pot . . . freeing up your oven, or even eliminating the need for your oven in most cases.

So, don't stress about what you're going to make this holiday! Your favorite Fix-It and Forget-It community has come together once again, to make all your holiday food wishes come true!

What Is an Instant Pot?

In short, an Instant Pot is a digital pressure cooker that also has multiple other functions. Not only can it be used as a pressure cooker, but depending on which model Instant Pot you have, you can set it to do things like sauté, cook rice, grains, porridge, soup/stew, beans/chili, porridge, meat, poultry, cake, eggs, yogurt. You can use the Instant Pot to steam or slow cook or even set it manually. Because the Instant Pot has so many functions, it takes away the need for multiple appliances on your counter and allows you to use fewer pots and pans.

Getting Started with Your Instant Pot

Get to Know Your Instant Pot . . .

The very first thing most Instant Pot owners do is called the water test. It helps you get to know your Instant Pot a bit, familiarizes you with it, and might even take a bit of your apprehension away (because if you're anything like me, I was scared to death to use it).

Step 1: Plug in your Instant Pot. This may seem obvious to some, but when we're nervous about using a new appliance, sometimes we forget things like this.

Step 2: Make sure the inner pot is inserted in the cooker. You should *never* attempt to cook anything in your device without the inner pot, or you will ruin your Instant Pot. Food should never come into contact with the actual housing unit.

Step 3: The inner pot has lines for each cup. Fill the inner pot with water until it reaches the 3-cup line.

Step 4: Check the sealing ring to be sure it's secure and in place. You should not be able to move it around. If it's not in place properly, you may experience issues with the pot letting out a lot of steam while cooking, or not coming to pressure.

Step 5: Seal the lid. There is an arrow on the lid between and "open" and "close." There is also an arrow on the top of the base of the Instant Pot between a picture of a locked lock and an unlocked lock. Line those arrows up, then turn the lid toward the picture of the lock (left).You will hear a noise that will indicate the lid is locked. If you do not hear a noise, it's not locked. Try it again.

Step 6: *Always* check to see if the steam valve on top of the lid is turned to "sealing." If it's not on "sealing" and is on "venting," it will not be able to come to pressure.

Step 7: Press the "Steam" button and use the +/- arrow to set it to 2 minutes. Once it's at the desired time, you don't need to press anything else. In a few seconds, the Instant Pot will begin all on its own. For those of us with digital slow cookers, we have a tendency to look for the "start" button, but there isn't one on the Instant Pot.

Step 8: Now you wait for the "magic" to happen! The cooking will begin once the device comes to pressure. This can take anywhere from 5 to 30 minutes, in my experience. Then, you will see the countdown happen (from the time you set it for). After that, the Instant Pot will beep, which means your meal is done!

Step 9: Your Instant Pot will now automatically switch to "warm" and begin a count of how many minutes it's been on warm. The next part is where you either wait for the NPR, or natural pressure release (the pressure releases on its own) or do what's called a QR, or quick release (you manually release the pressure). Which method you choose depends on what you're cooking, but in this case, you can choose either, because it's just water. For NPR, you will wait for the lever to move all the way back over to "venting" and watch the pinion (float valve) next to the lever. It will be flush with the lid when at full pressure and will drop when the pressure is done releasing. If you choose QR, be very careful not to have your hands over the vent, as the steam is very hot and you can burn yourself.

The Three Most Important Buttons You Need to Know About

You will find the majority of recipes will use the following three buttons:

Manual/Pressure Cook: Some older models tend to say "Manual," and the newer models seem to say "Pressure Cook." They mean the same thing. From here, you use the +/- button to change the cook time. After several seconds, the Instant Pot will begin its process. The exact name of this button will vary on your model of Instant Pot.

Sauté: Many recipes will have you sauté vegetables, or brown meat before beginning the pressure cooking process. For this setting, you will not use the lid of the Instant Pot.

Keep Warm/Cancel: This may just be the most important button on the Instant Pot. When you forget to use the +/- buttons to change the time for a recipe, or you press a wrong button, you can hit "keep warm/cancel" and it will turn your Instant Pot off for you.

What Do All the Buttons Do?

With so many buttons, it's hard to remember what each one does or means. You can use this as a quick guide in a pinch.

Soup/Broth. This button cooks at high pressure for 30 minutes. It can be adjusted using the +/- buttons to cook more, for 40 minutes, or less, for 20 minutes.

Meat/Stew. This button cooks at high pressure for 35 minutes. It can be adjusted using the +/- buttons to cook more, for 45 minutes, or less, for 20 minutes.

Bean/Chili. This button cooks at high pressure for 30 minutes. It can be adjusted using the +/- buttons to cook more, for 40 minutes, or less, for 25 minutes.

Poultry. This button cooks at high pressure for 15 minutes. It can be adjusted using the +/- buttons to cook more, for 30 minutes, or less, for 5 minutes.

Rice. This button cooks at low pressure and is the only fully automatic program. It is for cooking white rice and will automatically adjust the cooking time depending on the amount of water and rice in the cooking pot.

Multigrain. This button cooks at high pressure for 40 minutes. It can be adjusted using the +/- buttons to cook more, for 45 minutes of warm water soaking time and 60 minutes pressure cooking time, or less, for 20 minutes.

Porridge. This button cooks at high pressure for 20 minutes. It can be adjusted using the +/- buttons to cook more, for 30 minutes, or less, for 15 minutes.

Steam. This button cooks at High pressure for 10 minutes. It can be adjusted using the +/- buttons to cook more, for 15 minutes, or less, for 3 minutes. Always use a rack or steamer basket with this function, because it heats at full power continuously while it's coming to pressure, and you do not want food in direct contact with the bottom of the pressure cooking pot or it will burn. Once it reaches pressure, the steam button regulates pressure by cycling on and off, similar to the other pressure buttons.

Less | Normal | More. Adjust between the *Less | Normal | More* settings by pressing the same cooking function button repeatedly until you get to the desired setting. (Older versions use the *Adjust* button.)

+/- Buttons. Adjust the cook time up [+] or down [-]. (On newer models, you can also press and hold [-] or [+] for 3 seconds to turn sound OFF or ON.)

Cake. This button cooks at high pressure for 30 minutes. It can be adjusted using the +/- buttons to cook more, for 40 minutes, or less, for 25 minutes.

Egg. This button cooks at high pressure for 5 minutes. It can be adjusted using the +/- buttons to cook more, for 6 minutes, or less, for 4 minutes.

Instant Pot Tips and Tricks and Other Things You May Not Know

- Never attempt to cook directly in the Instant Pot without the inner pot!
- Once you set the time, you can walk away. It will show the time you set it to, then will change to the word "on" while the pressure builds. Once the Instant Pot has come to pressure, you will once again see the time you set it for. It will count down from there.
- Always make sure the sealing ring is securely in place. If it shows signs of wear or tear, it needs to be replaced.
- Have a sealing ring for savory recipes and a separate sealing ring for sweet recipes. Many people report their desserts tasting like a roast (or another savory food) if they try to use the same sealing ring for all recipes.
- The stainless steel rack (trivet) the Instant Pot comes with can used to keep food from being completely submerged in liquid, like baked potatoes or ground beef. It can also be used to set another pot on, for pot-in-pot cooking.
- If you use warm or hot liquid instead of cold liquid, you may need to adjust the cooking time, or the food may not come out done.
- Always double-check to see that the valve on the lid is set to "sealing" and not "venting" when you first lock the lid. This will save you from the Instant Pot not coming to pressure.
- Use Natural Pressure Release for tougher cuts of meat, recipes with high starch (like rice or grains), and recipes with a high volume of liquid. This means you let the Instant Pot naturally release pressure. The little bobbin will fall once pressure is released completely.

- Use Quick Release for more delicate cuts of meat, such as seafood and chicken breasts, and for steaming vegetables. This means you manually turn the vent (being careful not to put your hand over the vent) to release the pressure. The little bobbin will fall once pressure is released completely.
- Make sure there is a clear pathway for the steam to release. The last thing you want is to ruin the bottom of your cupboards with all that steam.
- You *must* use liquid in the Instant Pot. The *minimum* amount of liquid you should have in the inner pot is ½ cup, but most recipes work best with at least 1 cup.
- Do *not* overfill the Instant Pot! It should only be ½ full for rice or beans (food that expands greatly when cooked), or ⅔ of the way full for almost everything else. Do not fill it to the max fill line.
- In this book, the cook time *does not* take into account the amount of time it will take the Instant Pot to come to pressure, or the amount of time it will take the Instant Pot to release pressure. Be aware of this when choosing a recipe to make.
- If the Instant Pot is not coming to pressure, it's usually because the sealing ring is not on properly, or the vent is not set to "sealing."
- The more liquid, or the colder the ingredients, the longer it will take for the Instant Pot to come to pressure.
- Always make sure that the Instant Pot is dry before inserting the inner pot, and make sure the inner pot is dry before inserting it into the Instant Pot.
- Use a binder clip to hold the inner pot tight against the outer pot when sautéing and stirring. This will keep the pot from "spinning" in the base.
- Doubling a recipe does not change the cook time, but instead it will take longer to come up to pressure.
- You do not always need to double the liquid when doubling a recipe. Depending on what you're making, more liquid may make the food too watery. Use your best judgment.
- When using the slow cooker function, use the following chart:

Slow Cooker	Instant Pot
Warm	Less or Low
Low	Normal or Medium
High	More or High

Instant Pot Accessories

Most Instant Pots come with a stainless steel trivet. Below, you will find a list of accessories that will be used in this cookbook. Most of these accessories can be purchased in-store or online.

- Trivet and/or steamer basket—stainless steel or silicone
- 7-inch nonstick or silicone springform cake pan or 7-inch round baking pan
- 7-inch Bundt cake pan
- Sling or trivet with handles
- 1½-quart round baking dish

Breakfasts

Cinnamon French Toast Casserole

Hope Comerford, Clinton Township, MI

Makes 8 servings
Prep. Time: 10 minutes ⚜ Cook Time: 20 minutes

3 eggs

2 cups milk

¼ cup maple syrup

1 tsp. vanilla extract

1 tsp. cinnamon

Pinch salt

16-oz. loaf cinnamon swirl bread, cubed and left out overnight to go stale

Nonstick cooking spray

1 cup water

1. In a medium bowl, whisk together the eggs, milk, maple syrup, vanilla, cinnamon, and salt. Stir in the cubes of cinnamon swirl bread.

2. You will need a 7-inch round pan for this. Spray the inside with nonstick cooking spray, then pour the bread mixture into the pan.

3. Place the trivet in the bottom of the inner pot, then pour in the water.

4. Make a foil sling and insert it onto the trivet. Carefully place the 7-inch pan on top of the foil sling/trivet.

5. Secure the lid to the locked position, then make sure the vent is turned to sealing.

6. Press the Manual button and use the "+/-" button to set the Instant Pot for 20 minutes.

7. When the cook time is over, let the Instant Pot release naturally for 5 minutes, then quick release the rest.

Serving suggestion:
Serve with whipped cream and fresh fruit on top, with an extra sprinkle of cinnamon.

Quick and Easy Instant Pot Cinnamon Rolls

Hope Comerford, Clinton Township, MI

Makes 5 servings
Prep. Time: 5 minutes ⚜ Cook Time: 13 minutes

2 cups water

17-oz. can Pillsbury Grands! Original Cinnamon Rolls with Icing

1. Place the water in the inner pot of the Instant Pot, then place the trivet inside.

2. Cover the trivet with aluminum foil so that it also wraps up the sides.

3. Grease a 7-inch round pan and arrange the cinnamon rolls inside. Set the icing aside. Place this pan on top of the aluminum foil inside the inner pot.

4. Secure the lid and make sure the vent is in the sealed position. Press Manual, high pressure for 13 minutes.

5. Release the pressure manually when cooking time is up.

6. Remove the lid carefully so that the moisture does not drip on the cinnamon rolls.

7. Drizzle the icing on top of the cinnamon rolls and serve.

Pumpkin Spice Pancake Bites

Hope Comerford, Clinton Township, MI

Makes 14 pancake bites
Prep. Time: 10 minutes & Cook Time: 14 minutes

1 cup gluten-free cup-for-cup flour
1 tsp. baking powder
½ tsp. baking soda
½ tsp. cinnamon
¼ tsp. ground ginger
¼ tsp. nutmeg
Pinch salt
¾ cup pumpkin puree
1 cup unsweetened almond milk
1 tsp. vanilla extract
1 large egg, beaten
Nonstick cooking spray
1 ½ cups water

1. In a mixing bowl, combine the gluten-free flour, baking powder, baking soda, cinnamon, ginger, nutmeg, and salt.

2. Stir in the pumpkin, almond milk, vanilla, and egg until all ingredients are well-mixed.

3. Spray 2 silicone egg bite molds with nonstick cooking spray. Place 2 tablespoons of batter into each cup of the molds. Cover each filled egg bite mold tightly with foil.

4. Pour 1½ cups of water into the bottom of the Instant Pot and set the trivet on top.

5. Stack the filled silicone egg molds onto one another on top of the trivet in the inner pot.

6. Secure the lid and set the vent to sealing.

7. With the Manual setting, set the cook time to 14 minutes on high pressure.

8. When the cook time is over, let the pressure release naturally for 5 minutes, then manually release the rest of the pressure.

9. Carefully remove the trivet with oven mitts, uncover the egg bite molds, and pop out the pancake bites onto a plate or serving platter.

Serving suggestion:

Serve alongside some apple slices and with a bit of maple syrup for dipping the Pumpkin Spice Pancake Bites in.

Banana Bread Bites

Hope Comerford, Clinton Township, MI

Makes 14 banana bread bites
Prep. Time: 10 minutes & Cook Time: 10 minutes

1½ cups gluten-free cup-for-cup flour

½ cup gluten-free old-fashioned oats

1 tsp. baking soda

½ tsp. cinnamon

¼ tsp. nutmeg

¼ tsp. salt

3 very ripe bananas, mashed

⅓ cup unsweetened applesauce

½ cup honey

2 eggs

1 tsp. vanilla extract

1 cup water

1. In a bowl, mix together the flour, oats, baking soda, cinnamon, nutmeg, and salt.

2. In a separate bowl, mix together the mashed bananas, applesauce, honey, eggs, and vanilla.

3. Mix the wet ingredients into the dry ingredients, only until just combined. Do not overmix.

4. Spray 2 silicone egg bite molds with nonstick cooking spray.

5. Fill each mold ¾ of the way full of batter. Cover the molds with foil.

6. Pour 1 cup of water into the inner pot of the Instant Pot.

7. Stack both filled silicone molds onto the trivet and carefully lower the trivet into the inner pot.

8. Secure the lid and set the vent to sealing.

9. Manually select 10 minutes of cooking time on high pressure.

10. When the cook time is over, let the pressure release naturally for 5 minutes, then manually release the remaining pressure.

11. Remove the lid and carefully lift the trivet and molds out of the pot with oven mitts.

12. Remove the foil and allow the banana bread bites to cool. Pop them out of the molds onto a plate or serving platter.

Apple Cranberry Muffin Bites

Hope Comerford, Clinton Township, MI

Makes 14 muffin bites
Prep. Time: 10 minutes   *Cook Time: 13 minutes*

1⅓ cups whole wheat flour

⅓ cup brown sugar

2 tsp. baking powder

½ tsp. baking soda

½ tsp. cinnamon

2 eggs, or 4 egg whites

¼ cup unsweetened applesauce

1 tsp. orange zest

1 Tbsp. freshly squeezed orange juice

1 cup nonfat plain Greek yogurt

1 large Granny Smith apple, peeled and shredded

½ cup fresh, or frozen and unthawed, cranberries cut in half

Nonstick cooking spray

1 cup water

1. Mix the whole wheat flour, brown sugar, baking powder, baking soda, and cinnamon together in a bowl.

2. In a separate bowl, mix the eggs, applesauce, orange zest, orange juice, and Greek yogurt.

3. Gently fold in the shredded apples and cranberries.

4. Spray 2 silicone egg bite molds with nonstick cooking spray.

5. Fill each mold ¾ of the way full of batter. Cover the molds with foil.

6. Pour 1 cup of the water into the inner pot of the Instant Pot.

7. Stack both filled silicone molds onto the trivet and carefully lower the trivet into the inner pot.

8. Secure the lid and set the vent to sealing.

9. Manually select 13 minutes of cooking time on high pressure.

10. When the cook time is over, let the pressure release naturally for 10 minutes, then manually release the remaining pressure.

11. Remove the lid and carefully lift the trivet and molds out of the pot with oven mitts.

12. Remove the foil and allow the muffins to cool. Pop them out of the molds onto a plate or serving platter.

Christmas Morning Breakfast Casserole

Hope Comerford, Clinton Township, MI

Makes 4–6 servings
Prep. Time: 15 minutes   ⚜   Cook Time: 25 minutes

1 Tbsp. olive oil

½ lb. bulk breakfast sausage

½ cup finely diced onion

1 cup water

Nonstick cooking spray

½ lb. frozen Tater Tots or hash browns

6 eggs

¼ cup half-and-half

½ tsp. salt

½ tsp. garlic powder

¼ tsp. black pepper

⅛ tsp. cayenne pepper

½ cup diced bell pepper (any color you wish)

1 cup shredded pepper Jack cheese

½ cup shredded cheddar cheese

Variation:

You can use any types of cheese that your family likes. You do not have to stick with what is suggested above. Also, you could use bacon instead of sausage, or omit the meat altogether.

1. Set the Instant Pot to the Sauté function and add the olive oil.

2. Add the bulk sausage and onion to the inner pot of the Instant Pot and cook until browned. Remove it from the Instant Pot and set aside. Press the Cancel button.

3. Carefully wipe out the inside of the Instant Pot. Pour in the water and scrape the bottom, to be sure there is nothing stuck. Place the trivet on top with handles up.

4. Grease a 7-inch baking pan with butter or nonstick cooking spray. Arrange the Tater Tots or hash browns evenly around the bottom of the pan.

5. In a bowl, mix together the eggs, half-and-half, salt, garlic powder, black pepper, and cayenne. Stir in the bell pepper and pepper jack cheese. Pour this over the hash browns.

6. Sprinkle the cheddar over the top of the casserole. Cover with foil. Carefully lower the baking pan onto the trivet.

7. Secure the lid and set the vent to sealing. Manually set the cook time for 25 minutes on high pressure.

8. When the cook time is over, let the pressure release naturally for 10 minutes, then manually release the remaining pressure.

9. With hot pads, carefully remove the baking pan with the handles of the trivet. Uncover, serve, and enjoy!

Garden Vegetable Crustless Quiche

Susan Kasting, Jenks, OK

Makes 4 servings
Prep. Time: 20 minutes ⚜ Cook Time: 25 minutes ⚜ Standing Time: 10 minutes

1½ cups water

1½ cups egg substitute

3 large eggs

⅓ cup skim milk

½ cup whole wheat pastry flour

8 oz. low-sodium fat-free cottage cheese

2 medium zucchini, sliced

½ small onion, diced

1 green bell pepper, finely chopped

½ lb. fresh mushrooms, sliced

½ cup chopped parsley

Nonstick cooking spray

1 tomato, sliced

1 cup low-fat shredded cheese of your choice

1. Pour the water into the inner pot of the Instant Pot and place the trivet on top.

2. In a large bowl, beat the egg substitute and eggs until fluffy.

3. Stir in the milk, flour, and cottage cheese.

4. Sauté the zucchini, onion, bell pepper, and mushrooms in a pan coated with cooking spray for 5 minutes.

5. Stir the sautéed vegetable mixture and parsley into the egg mixture.

6. When well combined, pour into a 7-inch round baking dish, lightly coated with cooking spray.

7. Top with tomato slices and cheese. Cover tightly with foil.

8. Place the baking pan on top of the trivet in the Instant Pot.

9. Secure the lid and set the vent to sealing.

10. Manually set the time for 25 minutes on high pressure.

11. When the cook time is over, allow the pressure to release naturally for 10 minutes, then manually release the remaining pressure.

12. When the pin drops, remove the lid, and carefully remove the trivet with oven mitts. Carefully remove the foil. Allow the quiche to stand for 10 minutes before slicing.

Delicious Shirred Eggs

Hope Comerford, Clinton Township, MI

Makes 6 servings
Prep. Time: 5 minutes & Cook Time: 2–3 minutes

Nonstick cooking spray
2 Tbsp. fresh minced onion
1 garlic clove, minced
6 Tbsp. skim milk, *divided*
6 jumbo eggs
6 Tbsp. fresh Parmesan cheese, grated, *divided*
Fresh cracked pepper
1 cup water

1. Spray 6 ramekins with nonstick cooking spray.

2. Evenly divide the minced onion and garlic between the 6 ramekins.

3. Pour 1 tablespoon of milk into each ramekin.

4. Break an egg into each ramekin.

5. Top each egg with 1 tablespoon freshly grated cheese.

6. Season with fresh cracked pepper.

7. Pour the water into the bottom of the Instant Pot. Place the trivet on top.

8. Arrange 3 ramekins on top of the trivet, then carefully stack the remaining 3 ramekins on top, staggering their positions to each ramekin on top is sitting between 2 on the bottom layer.

9. Secure the lid and set the vent to sealing.

10. Set the Instant Pot to low pressure and manually set the cook time to 2 minutes for runny yolks or 3 minutes for hard yolks.

11. When the cook time is over, manually release the pressure and remove the lid. Serve immediately.

Soups, Stews & Chilies

Chicken Noodle Soup

Colleen Heatwole, Burton, MI

Makes 6–8 servings
Prep. Time: 15 minutes   &   Cook Time: 4 minutes

2 Tbsp. butter

1 Tbsp. oil

1 medium onion, diced

2 large carrots, diced

3 celery stalks, diced

Salt to taste

3 garlic cloves, minced

1 tsp. thyme

1 tsp. oregano

1 tsp. basil

8 cups chicken broth

2 cups cubed cooked chicken

8 oz. medium egg noodles

1 cup peas (if frozen, thaw while preparing soup)

Pepper to taste

1. In the inner pot of the Instant Pot, melt the butter with oil on the Sauté function.

2. Add the onion, carrots, and celery with a large pinch of salt and continue cooking on Sauté until soft, about 5 minutes, stirring frequently.

3. Add the garlic, thyme, oregano, and basil and sauté an additional minute.

4. Add the broth, cooked chicken, and noodles, stirring to combine all ingredients.

5. Put the lid on the Instant Pot and set the vent to sealing. Select Manual high pressure and add 4 minutes.

6. When time is up do a quick (manual) release of the pressure.

7. Add the thawed peas, stir, adjust seasoning with salt and pepper, and serve.

Turkey Frame Soup

Joyce Zuercher, Hesston, KS

Makes 6–8 servings
Prep. Time: 20 minutes ⚓ Cook Time: 5 minutes

1 Tbsp. olive oil

1 onion, diced

4 cups chopped fresh vegetables—any combination of sliced celery, carrots, onions, rutabaga, broccoli, cauliflower, mushrooms, and more

3 qt. turkey broth, *divided*

2–3 cups cooked and cut-up turkey

16-oz. can chopped tomatoes

1 Tbsp. chicken bouillon granules

1 tsp. dried thyme

½ –¾ tsp. salt, or to taste

⅛ tsp. pepper

1½ tsp. dried oregano

1½ cups uncooked noodles

1. Set the Instant Pot to the Sauté function and heat the olive oil.

2. Once the oil is heated, add the onion to the inner pot and sauté for about 3 minutes.

3. Add the rest of the veggies and continue to sauté for an additional 5 minutes.

4. Add 1 cup of the turkey broth and scrape the bottom of the inner pot with a wooden spoon or spatula. Press Cancel.

5. Add the remaining broth, along with the turkey, chopped tomatoes, bouillon, and seasonings.

6. Secure the lid and set the vent to sealing. Manually set the cook time for 5 minutes on high pressure.

7. When the cook time is over, manually release the pressure.

8. When the pin drops, remove the lid and press Cancel. Then, press the Sauté function. Stir in the noodles and let them cook for about 4 minutes.

9. When the noodles are done to your liking, press Cancel. Serve and enjoy!

Turkey Peasant Soup

Alice Valine, Elma, NY

Makes 8 servings
Prep. Time: 11 minutes   &   Cook Time: 5 minutes

2 Tbsp. olive oil

I medium onion, chopped

2–3 cloves garlic, minced

½ lb. bulk turkey sausage

2 (15-oz.) cans cannellini beans, rinsed and drained

2 (14½-oz.) cans no-salt-added diced tomatoes

4 cups low-sodium chicken or vegetable stock

2 tsp. Italian seasoning

3 medium zucchini, sliced

4 cups fresh spinach leaves, chopped, or whole-leaf baby spinach

Shredded Parmesan or Romano, cheese, *optional*

1. Set the Instant Pot to Sauté and heat the olive oil in the inner pot.

2. Sauté the onion and garlic for about 3 minutes. Push it to the outer edges and brown the turkey sausage for an additional 5 to 8 minutes.

3. Press Cancel and add the cannellini beans, diced tomatoes, chicken stock, Italian seasoning, and zucchini.

4. Secure the lid and set the vent to sealing.

5. Manually set the cook time for 5 minutes on high pressure.

6. When the cook time is over, let the pressure release naturally for 10 minutes, then manually release the remaining pressure.

7. When the pin drops, remove the lid and stir in the spinach. Allow the spinach to wilt.

8. Serve each bowl with an optional sprinkle of shredded Parmesan or Romano cheese.

Leftover Turkey Tortilla Soup

Hope Comerford, Clinton Township, MI

Makes 6–8 servings
Prep. Time: 10 minutes   Cook Time: 10 minutes

2 Tbsp. olive oil

¾ cup chopped red onion

2 cups chopped leftover turkey

2 carrots, diced

1 celery stalk, diced

1 jalapeño, seeded and diced

1½ tsp. cumin

1½ tsp. chili powder

1½ tsp. garlic powder

1½ tsp. onion powder

1 tsp. salt

¼ tsp. pepper

6 cups chicken or turkey stock

Juice of 1 or 2 limes

Toppings: chopped cilantro, sour cream, tortilla strips, avocado slices, shredded Mexican-blend cheese, *optional*

1. Set the Instant Pot to the Sauté function and heat the olive oil in the inner pot.

2. When the oil is heated, add the onion, and cook it for about 3 to 5 minutes, stirring frequently. Press Cancel on the Instant Pot when done.

3. Add the turkey, carrots, celery, jalapeño, cumin, chili powder, onion powder, garlic powder, salt, and pepper. Pour in the stock.

4. Secure the lid and set the vent to sealing. Manually set the cook time for 10 minutes.

5. When the cook time is over, let the pressure release naturally for a few minutes, then manually release the remaining pressure.

6. When the pin drops, remove the lid, and add the lime juice to your liking.

7. Serve while still hot with your desired assortment of toppings.

Turkey Meatball Soup

Mary Ann Lefever, Lancaster, PA

Makes 8 servings
Prep. Time: 10–20 minutes ⚬ *Cook Time: 14–15 minutes*

1 lb. ground turkey, uncooked

1 medium onion, diced, *divided*

2 large eggs, beaten

½ cup Italian bread crumbs

½ cup freshly grated Parmesan, plus more for serving

1 tsp. salt

¼ tsp. pepper

2 Tbsp. olive oil

4–5 large carrots, chopped

8 cups chicken broth, *divided*

¾ lb. escarole, washed and cut into bite-size pieces

Variation:

If you wish, you can substitute 3 cups cut-up cooked turkey for the ground turkey meatballs.

1. In a bowl, mix the ground turkey, ½ of the onion, eggs, bread crumbs, ½ cup Parmesan, the salt, and the pepper. Form into 1-inch meatballs.

2. Set the Instant Pot to Sauté. Heat the olive oil. Brown the meatballs on each side for 2 minutes. This may take you a couple batches. Remove the meatballs and set aside.

3. Add the remaining onion and carrots. Sauté for 3 to 5 minutes.

4. Pour in 1 cup of the broth and scrape the bottom of the inner pot with a wooden spoon or spatula. Press Cancel.

5. Pour the remaining broth in and gently drop the meatballs into the broth.

6. Secure the lid and set the vent to sealing. Manually set the cook time for 10 minutes on high pressure.

7. When the cook time is over, let the pressure release naturally for 2 minutes, then release the remaining pressure.

8. When the pin drops, remove the lid. Press Cancel, then press Sauté. Stir in the escarole. Allow the escarole to wilt, about 4 to 5 minutes.

9. Serve hot sprinkled with extra Parmesan cheese.

Beef Mushroom Barley Soup

Becky Frey, Lebanon, PA

Makes 8 servings
Prep. Time: 20 minutes   ⚜   Cook Time: 25 minutes

2 Tbsp. olive oil, *divided*

1 lb. boneless beef chuck, cubed

1 large onion, chopped

2 cloves garlic, crushed

1 lb. fresh mushrooms, sliced

1 celery stalk, sliced

2 carrots, sliced

½ tsp. dried thyme, *optional*

8 cups low-sodium beef stock

½ cup uncooked pearl barley

½ tsp. freshly ground pepper

3 Tbsp. chopped fresh parsley

1. Set the Instant Pot to the Sauté function and heat 1 tablespoon of the olive oil in the inner pot.

2. Brown the beef, in batches if needed, and then remove and set aside.

3. Add the remaining tablespoon of olive oil and sauté the onion, garlic, and mushrooms for 3 to 4 minutes.

4. Add the beef back in, as well as all the remaining ingredients, except for the parsley. Press Cancel.

5. Secure the lid and set the vent to sealing.

6. Manually set the cook time to 25 minutes on high pressure.

7. When the cook time is over, let the pressure release naturally for 15 minutes, then manually release the remaining pressure.

8. When the pin drops, remove the lid and stir. Serve each bowl topped with some fresh chopped parsley.

Italian Vegetable Soup

Patti Boston, Newark, OH

Makes 6 servings
Prep. Time: 20 minutes & Cook Time: 10 minutes

3 small carrots, sliced

1 small onion, chopped

2 small potatoes, diced

2 Tbsp. chopped parsley

1 garlic clove, minced

3 tsp. sodium-free beef bouillon powder

1¼ tsp. dried basil

¼ tsp. pepper

16-oz. can red kidney beans, undrained

14½-oz. can stewed tomatoes, with juice

1 cup diced, extra-lean, lower-sodium cooked ham

3 cups water

1. In the inner pot of the Instant Pot, layer the carrots, onion, potatoes, parsley, garlic, beef bouillon, basil, pepper, kidney beans, stewed tomatoes, and ham. Do not stir. Add the water.

2. Secure the lid and set the vent to sealing. Manually set the cook time for 10 minutes.

3. When the cook time is over, let the pressure release naturally for 2 minutes, then manually release the remaining pressure.

Veggie Minestrone

Dorothy VanDeest, Memphis, TN

Makes 8 servings
Prep. Time: 5 minutes & Cook Time: 4 minutes

2 Tbsp. olive oil

1 large onion, chopped

1 garlic clove, minced

4 cups low-sodium chicken or vegetable stock

16-oz. can kidney beans, rinsed and drained

14½-oz. can no-salt-added diced tomatoes

2 medium carrots, sliced thin

¼ tsp. dried oregano

¼ tsp. pepper

½ cup whole wheat elbow macaroni, uncooked

4 oz. fresh spinach

½ cup grated Parmesan cheese

1. Set the Instant Pot to the Sauté function and heat the olive oil.

2. When the olive oil is heated, add the onion and garlic to the inner pot and sauté for 5 minutes.

3. Press Cancel and add the stock, kidney beans, diced tomatoes, carrots, oregano, and pepper. Gently pour in the macaroni, but *do not stir*. Just push the noodles gently under the liquid.

4. Secure the lid and set the vent to sealing.

5. Manually set the cook time for 4 minutes on high pressure.

6. When the cook time is over, manually release the pressure and remove the lid when the pin drops.

7. Stir in the spinach and let wilt a few minutes.

8. Sprinkle 1 tablespoon grated Parmesan on each individual bowl of the soup. Enjoy!

Potato Bacon Soup

Colleen Heatwole, Burton, MI

Makes 4–6 servings
Prep. Time: 30 minutes   ♣   Cook Time: 5 minutes

5 lb. potatoes, peeled and cubed

3 stalks of celery, diced into ¼-inch to ½-inch pieces

1 large onion, chopped

1 clove garlic, minced

1 Tbsp. seasoning salt

½ tsp. black pepper

4 cups chicken broth

1 lb. bacon, fried crisp and rough chopped

1 cup half-and-half

1 cup milk, 2% or whole

Sour cream, shredded cheddar cheese, and diced scallion to garnish, *optional*

1. Place the potatoes in the bottom of the inner pot.

2. Add the celery, onion, garlic, seasoning salt, and pepper, then stir to combine.

3. Add the chicken broth and bacon to the pot and stir to combine.

4. Secure the lid and make sure the vent is on sealing. Using Manual mode select 5 minutes, high pressure.

5. Manually release the pressure when cooking time is up. Open pot and roughly mash potatoes, leaving some large chunks if desired.

6. Add the half-and-half and milk.

7. Serve while still hot with your desired assortment of garnishes.

Split Pea Soup

Judy Gascho, Woodburn, OR

Makes 3–4 servings
Prep. Time: 20 minutes ⚘ *Cook Time: 15 minutes*

4 cups chicken broth

4 sprigs thyme

4 oz. ham, diced (about ⅓ cup)

2 Tbsp. butter

2 stalks celery

2 carrots

1 large leek

3 cloves garlic

1 cup dried green split peas (about 12 oz.)

Salt to taste

Pepper to taste

1. Pour the broth into the inner pot of the Instant Pot and set to Sauté. Add the thyme, ham, and butter.

2. While the broth heats, chop the celery and cut the carrots into ½-inch-thick rounds. Halve the leek lengthwise and thinly slice and chop the garlic. Add the vegetables to the pot as you cut them. Rinse the split peas in a colander, discarding any stones, then add to the pot.

3. Secure the lid, making sure the steam valve is in the sealing position. Set the cooker to Manual at high pressure for 15 minutes. When the time is up, carefully turn the steam valve to the venting position to release the pressure manually.

4. Turn off the Instant Pot. Remove the lid and stir the soup; discard the thyme sprigs.

5. Thin the soup with up to 1 cup of water if needed (the soup will continue to thicken as it cools). Season with salt and pepper.

Creamy Wild Rice Mushroom Soup

Hope Comerford, Clinton Township, MI

Makes 4–6 servings
Prep. Time: 10 minutes ⚘ *Cook Time: 40 minutes*

½ large onion, chopped

3 cloves garlic, chopped

3 celery stalks, chopped

3 carrots, chopped

8 oz. fresh baby bella mushrooms, sliced

1 cup wild rice

4 cups low-sodium chicken or vegetable stock

½ tsp. dried thyme

¼ tsp. pepper

1 cup fat-free half-and-half, heated

2 Tbsp. cornstarch

2 Tbsp. cold water

1. Place the onion, garlic, celery, carrots, mushrooms, wild rice, stock, thyme, and pepper in the inner pot of the Instant Pot and secure the lid. Make sure the vent is set to sealing.

2. Manually set the time for 30 minutes on high pressure.

3. When the cook time is over, manually release the pressure and remove the lid when the pin drops.

4. While the pressure is releasing, heat the half-in-half either in the microwave or on the stovetop.

5. Whisk together the cornstarch and cold water. Whisk this into the heated half-and-half.

6. Slowly whisk the half-and-half/cornstarch mixture into the soup in the Instant Pot. Serve and enjoy!

Butternut Squash Soup

Colleen Heatwole, Burton, MI

Makes 4 servings
Prep. Time: 30 minutes ⚲ *Cook Time: 15 minutes*

2 Tbsp. butter

1 large onion, chopped

2 cloves garlic, minced

1 tsp. thyme

½ tsp. sage

Salt to taste

Pepper to taste

2 large butternut squash, peeled, seeded, and cubed (about 4 lb.)

4 cups chicken stock

1. In the inner pot of the Instant Pot, melt the butter using Sauté function.

2. Add the onion and garlic and cook until soft, 3 to 5 minutes.

3. Add the thyme and sage and cook for another minute. Season with salt and pepper.

4. Stir in the butternut squash and add the chicken stock.

5. Secure the lid and make sure the vent is on sealing. Using the Manual setting, cook the squash and seasonings for 10 minutes, using high pressure.

6. When time is up, do a quick release of the pressure.

7. Puree the soup in a food processor or use an immersion blender right in the inner pot. If soup is too thick, add more stock. Adjust salt and pepper as needed.

French Onion Soup

Jenny R. Unternahrer, Wayland, IA
Janice Yoskovich, Carmichaels, PA

Makes 10 servings
Prep. Time: 10 minutes   &   Cook Time: 20 minutes

½ cup light, soft tub margarine

8–10 large onions, sliced

3 (14-oz.) cans 98% fat-free, lower-sodium beef broth

2½ cups water

3 tsp. sodium-free chicken bouillon powder

1½ tsp. Worcestershire sauce

3 bay leaves

10 (1-oz.) slices French bread, toasted

1. Turn the Instant Pot to the Sauté function and add the margarine and onions. Cook about 5 minutes, or until the onions are slightly soft. Press Cancel.

2. Add the beef broth, water, bouillon powder, Worcestershire sauce, and bay leaves and stir.

3. Secure the lid and make sure the vent is on sealing. Cook on Manual mode for 20 minutes.

4. Let the pressure release naturally for 15 minutes, then do a quick release. Open the lid and discard bay leaves.

5. Ladle into bowls. Top each with a slice of bread and some cheese if you desire.

Cream of Broccoli Soup

Hope Comerford, Clinton Township, MI

Makes 4 servings
Prep. Time: 10 minutes 🔹 Cook Time: 5 minutes

2 Tbsp. butter or margarine

1 medium onion, chopped

2 cloves garlic, chopped

1 lb. (about 5 cups) chopped fresh broccoli

4 cups chicken, or vegetable stock

½ tsp. salt

¼ tsp. pepper

2 Tbsp. cornstarch

1 cup heavy cream, *divided*

½ cup shredded cheddar cheese

1. Set the Instant Pot to Sauté and melt the butter.

2. When the butter is melted, sauté the onion and garlic for 5 minutes.

3. Press Cancel and add the broccoli, stock, salt, and pepper.

4. Secure the lid and set the vent to sealing.

5. Manually set the cook time to 5 minutes on high pressure.

6. When the cook time is over, manually release the pressure.

7. When the pin drops, remove the lid and use a potato smasher to break up the broccoli a bit and thicken the soup.

8. In a small dish, mix the cornstarch with a bit of the heavy cream until smooth. Then, whisk the cornstarch/heavy cream with the remaining heavy cream and *slowly* whisk this mixture into the soup.

9. Serve each bowl with a sprinkle of shredded cheddar cheese and enjoy!

White Chicken Chili

Judy Gascho, Woodburn, OR

Makes 6 servings
Prep. Time: 20 minutes ⚷ *Cook Time: 30 minutes*

2 Tbsp. cooking oil

1 ½ –2 lb. boneless chicken breasts or thighs

1 medium onion, chopped

3 cloves garlic, minced

2 cups chicken broth

3 (15-oz.) cans great northern beans, undrained

15-oz. can white corn, drained

4½-oz. can chopped green chilies, undrained

1 tsp. cumin

½ tsp. ground oregano

1 cup sour cream

1 cup grated cheddar or Mexican blend cheese

1. Set Instant Pot to Sauté and allow the inner pot to get hot.

2. Add the oil and chicken. Brown chicken on both sides.

3. Add the onion, garlic, chicken broth, undrained beans, drained corn, undrained green chilies, cumin, and oregano.

4. Place lid on and close valve to sealing.

5. Set to Bean/Chili for 30 minutes.

6. Let pressure release naturally for 15 minutes before carefully releasing any remaining steam.

7. Remove the chicken and shred.

8. Put the chicken, sour cream, and cheese in the inner pot. Stir until the cheese is melted.

Serving suggestion:

Serve with chopped cilantro and additional cheese.

Turkey Chili

Reita F. Yoder, Carlsbad, NM

Makes 8 servings
Prep. Time: 20 minutes ⚘ *Cook Time: 5 minutes*

Olive oil or nonstick cooking spray

2 lb. ground turkey

1 small onion, chopped

1 garlic clove, minced

16-oz. can low-sodium pinto or kidney beans

2 cups chopped fresh tomatoes

2 cups no-salt-added tomato sauce

16-oz. can RO-TEL tomatoes

1-oz. package low-sodium chili seasoning

1. Turn the Instant Pot to Sauté and add a touch of olive oil or cooking spray to the inner pot. Crumble the ground turkey in the inner pot and brown on the Sauté setting until cooked. Add the onion and garlic and sauté an additional 5 minutes, stirring constantly.

2. Add remaining ingredients to inner pot and mix well.

3. Secure the lid and make sure the vent is set to sealing. Cook on Manual for 5 minutes.

4. When the cook time is over, let the pressure release naturally for 10 minutes, then manually release the rest.

Serving suggestion:
Sprinkle with shredded cheddar cheese and chopped fresh cilantro.

Favorite Chili

Carol Eveleth, Cheyenne, WY

Makes 4–6 servings
Prep. Time: 10 minutes ⚹ Cook Time: 35 minutes

1 lb. ground beef
1 tsp. salt
½ tsp. black pepper
1 Tbsp. olive oil
1 small onion, chopped
2 cloves garlic, minced
1 green bell pepper, chopped
2 Tbsp. chili powder
½ tsp. cumin
1 cup water
16-oz. can chili beans, undrained
15-oz. can crushed tomatoes

1. Press the Sauté button and adjust once to Sauté More function. Wait until indicator says "hot."

2. Season the ground beef with salt and black pepper.

3. Add the olive oil to the inner pot. Coat the whole bottom of the pot with the oil.

4. Add the ground beef to the inner pot. The ground beef will start to release moisture. Allow the ground beef to brown and crisp slightly, stirring occasionally to break it up. Taste and adjust the seasoning with more salt and ground black pepper.

5. Add the onion, garlic, bell pepper, chili powder, and cumin. Sauté for about 5 minutes, until the spices start to release their fragrance. Stir frequently.

6. Add the water and the chili beans, not drained. Mix well. Pour in the tomatoes.

7. Close and secure the lid, making sure the vent is set to sealing, and pressure cook on Manual at high pressure for 10 minutes.

8. Let the pressure release naturally when cooking time is up. Open the lid carefully.

Serving suggestions:

Garnish chili with sour cream, shredded cheese, avocado pieces, jalapeño slices, or chopped onions.

Ground Turkey Stew

Carol Eveleth, Cheyenne, WY

Makes 4–6 servings
Prep. Time: 5 minutes & Cook Time: 25 minutes

1 Tbsp. oil

1 onion, chopped

½ tsp. salt

1 lb. ground turkey

½ tsp. garlic powder

1 tsp. chili powder

¾ tsp. cumin

2 tsp. coriander

1 tsp. dried oregano

1 green bell pepper, chopped

1 red bell pepper, chopped

1 tomato, chopped

1 cup tomato sauce

1 Tbsp. soy sauce

1 cup water

2 handfuls cilantro, chopped

15-oz. can black beans

Serving suggestion:

Serve with chopped avocado, green onions, cheese, or sour cream.

1. Press the Sauté function on the control panel of the Instant Pot.

2. Add the oil to the inner pot and let it get hot. Add onion, season with the salt, and sauté for a few minutes, or until light golden.

3. Add the ground turkey. Break the ground meat using a wooden spoon to avoid formation of lumps. Sauté for a few minutes, until the pink color has faded.

4. Add the garlic powder, chili powder, cumin, coriander, dried oregano, and salt. Combine well. Add the green bell pepper, red bell pepper, and tomato. Combine well.

5. Add the tomato sauce, soy sauce, and water; combine well.

6. Close and secure the lid. Click on the Cancel key to cancel the Sauté mode. Make sure the pressure release valve on the lid is in the sealing position.

7. Click on Manual function first and then select high pressure. Click the + button and set the time to 15 minutes.

8. You can either have the steam release naturally (it will take around 20 minutes) or, after 10 minutes, turn the pressure release valve on the lid to venting and release steam. Be careful as the steam is very hot. After the pressure has released completely, open the lid.

9. If the stew is watery, turn on the Sauté function and let it cook for a few more minutes with the lid off.

10. Add the cilantro and black beans, combine well, and let cook for a few minutes.

Instantly Good Beef Stew

Hope Comerford, Clinton Township, MI

Makes 6 servings
Prep. Time: 20 minutes   Cook Time: 35 minutes

3 Tbsp. olive oil, *divided*

2 lb. stewing beef, cubed

2 cloves garlic, minced

I large onion, chopped

3 ribs celery, sliced

3 large potatoes, cubed

2–3 carrots, sliced

8 oz. no-salt-added tomato sauce

10 oz. low-sodium beef broth

2 tsp. Worcestershire sauce

¼ tsp. pepper

I bay leaf

1. Set the Instant Pot to the Sauté function, then add 1 tablespoon of the oil. Add ⅓ of the beef cubes and brown and sear all sides. Repeat this process twice more with the remaining oil and beef cubes. Set the beef aside.

2. Place the garlic, onion, and celery into the pot and sauté for a few minutes. Press Cancel.

3. Add the beef back in as well as all the remaining ingredients.

4. Secure the lid and make sure the vent is set to sealing. Choose Manual for 35 minutes.

5. When the cook time is over, let the pressure release naturally for 15 minutes, then release any remaining pressure manually.

6. Remove the lid, remove the bay leaf, then serve.

NOTE:

If you want the stew to be a bit thicker, remove some of the potatoes, mash, then stir them back through the stew.

Meme's Meatball Stew

Maxine Phaneuf, Washington, MI

Makes 6–8 servings
Prep. Time: 10 minutes ⚓ Cook Time: 15 minutes

Meatballs:

1½ lb. lean ground beef

1 pkg. onion soup mix

¾ cup Italian bread crumbs

1 egg

Stew:

7 cups water

11¾-oz. can condensed tomato soup

2½ carrots, peeled and chopped

2 potatoes, peeled and chopped

2 big handfuls of fresh green beans, chopped

1 medium onion, chopped

1–2 tsp. salt

½ tsp. pepper

2 tsp. onion powder

2 tsp. garlic powder

1. In a medium bowl, mix together the meatball ingredients and form into golf ball–size meatballs.

2. In the inner pot of the Instant Pot, add the stew ingredients. Carefully drop in the meatballs.

3. Secure the lid and set the vent to sealing. Manually set the cook time for 15 minutes on high pressure.

4. When the cook time is over, let the pressure release naturally for 10 minutes, then manually release the remaining pressure.

Serving suggestion:

Serve each bowl with grated Parmesan cheese and a side of crusty Italian bread with butter.

Lamb and Guinness Stew

Hope Comerford, Clinton Township, MI

Makes 6 servings
Prep. Time: 30 minutes ♣ Cook Time: 30 minutes

2½-lb. lamb shoulder, trimmed and cut into 1½-inch pieces

Salt to taste

Pepper to taste

2–3 Tbsp. olive oil

1 cup chopped onion

6 cloves garlic, chopped

1 cup Guinness

3 Tbsp. tomato paste

2 carrots, cut into ½-inch pieces on the diagonal

2 cups peeled and cubed Yukon Gold potatoes

1 bay leaf

1 sprig fresh rosemary

3 cups beef stock

1 cup water

1 cup frozen peas, thawed

¼ cup cornstarch

¼ cup cold water

1. Pat the lamb pieces dry and sprinkle with salt and pepper, to taste.

2. Set the Instant Pot to the Sauté function. Heat the olive oil in the inner pot, 1 tablespoon at a time. In batches, sear the lamb pieces on each side, adding more olive oil to the pot as needed. Set aside.

3. Pour the onion and garlic into the inner pot and sauté for 3 minutes or so.

4. Pour in the Guinness and scrape the bottom with a wooden spoon or spatula to bring up any bits.

5. Stir in the tomato paste, then add the lamb, carrots, potatoes, bay leaf, rosemary, beef stock, and water.

6. Secure the lid and set the vent to sealing. Manually set the cook time for 30 minutes on high pressure.

7. When the cook time is over, let the pressure release naturally for 10 minutes, then manually release the remaining pressure.

8. When the pin drops, remove the lid. Remove and discard the bay leaf.

9. Press cancel and then set the Instant Pot to the Sauté function. Pour in the peas.

10. In a small bowl, mix together the cornstarch and water. Stir it into the stew, allowing it to thicken. When the stew is thickened to your liking, press Cancel.

Main Dishes

Rotisserie Chicken

Hope Comerford, Clinton Township, MI

Makes 4 servings
Prep. Time: 5 minutes ⚶ *Cook Time: 33 minutes*

3-lb. whole chicken

2 Tbsp. olive oil, *divided*

Salt to taste

Pepper to taste

20–30 cloves fresh garlic, peeled and left whole

1 cup chicken stock, broth, or water

2 Tbsp. garlic powder

2 tsp. onion powder

½ tsp. basil

½ tsp. cumin

½ tsp. chili powder

1. Rub the chicken with 1 tablespoon of the olive oil and sprinkle with salt and pepper.

2. Place the garlic cloves inside the chicken. Use butcher's twine to secure the legs.

3. Press the Sauté button on the Instant Pot, then add the rest of the olive oil to the inner pot.

4. When the pot is hot, place the chicken inside. You are just trying to sear it, so leave it for about 4 minutes on each side.

5. Remove the chicken and set aside. Place the trivet at the bottom of the inner pot and pour in the chicken stock.

6. Mix together the remaining seasonings and rub them all over the entire chicken.

7. Place the chicken back inside the inner pot, breast-side up, on top of the trivet and secure the lid to the sealing position.

8. Press the Manual button and use the +/- to set it for 25 minutes.

9. When the timer beeps, allow the pressure to release naturally for 15 minutes. If the lid will not open at this point, quick release the remaining pressure and remove the chicken.

10. Let the chicken rest for 5–10 minutes before serving.

Skinny Chicken Stroganoff

Carol Sherwood, Batavia, NY

Makes 6 servings
Prep. Time: 10 minutes   ♣   Cook Time: 5 minutes

1 tsp. olive oil

1 cup chopped onion

1 clove garlic, pressed

1½ lb. boneless, skinless chicken breasts, cut into bite-size pieces

⅛ tsp. black pepper

8 oz. sliced fresh mushrooms

8 oz. uncooked whole wheat wide egg noodles

1 cup low-fat low-sodium chicken broth

¾ cup reduced-fat sour cream

4 slices turkey bacon, cooked and broken, *optional*

2 Tbsp. chopped fresh parsley, *optional*

2 Tbsp. cornstarch

2 Tbsp. cold water

1. Set the Instant Pot to Sauté and heat the olive oil in the inner pot.

2. Sauté the onion and garlic for 3 minutes. Press Cancel.

3. Add the chicken and pepper. Stir to coat everything in the pot. Pour the noodles on top. Evenly spread them out. Evenly spread the mushrooms on top of the noodles.

4. Pour the chicken broth on top. Secure the lid and set the vent to sealing.

5. Manually set the cook time for 2 minutes at high pressure.

6. When the cook time is over, let the pressure release naturally for 10 minutes, then manually release the remaining pressure.

7. When the pin drops, remove the lid. Stir.

8. Remove about ¼ cup of the liquid from the inner pot, and, in a separate bowl, mix this with the sour cream, tempering it. Slowly add this tempered sour cream to the inner pot, stirring constantly. Stir in the bacon and parsley if desired.

9. Set the Instant Pot to Sauté. In a small bowl, whisk together the cornstarch and water. Add this to the inner pot and stir. Cook for a couple of minutes, or until thickened to your liking, then press Cancel.

Chicken Alfredo

Hope Comerford, Clinton Township, MI

Makes 6–8 servings
Prep. Time: 5 minutes ⚖ *Cook Time: 5 minutes*

3 cups chicken broth

I cup white wine

I cup heavy cream

2 tsp. garlic powder

I ¼ tsp. sea salt, *divided*

I tsp. onion powder

¼ plus ⅛ tsp. pepper, *divided*

16 oz. uncooked fettuccine noodles, broken in half

2 Tbsp. butter, cut into pieces

I lb. boneless, skinless chicken thighs

I cup shredded Parmesan cheese

½ cup chopped flat-leaf parsley, for garnish

1. Pour the chicken broth, white wine, cream, garlic powder, 1 teaspoon of the sea salt, the onion powder and ¼ teaspoon pepper into the inner pot of the Instant Pot. Dump the pasta in and push the pasta under the liquid.

2. Arrange the butter over the top and then place the pieces of chicken on top of that and sprinkle with the remaining salt and pepper.

3. Secure the lid and set the vent to sealing. Manually set the cook time for 5 minutes on high pressure.

4. When the cook time is over, let the pressure release naturally for 10 minutes, then manually release the remaining pressure.

5. When the pin drops, remove the lid, then remove the chicken. You can either shred it, or cut it into strips. Stir back through the pasta.

6. Stir the Parmesan cheese through the pasta. Serve garnished with the parsley and enjoy!

Chicken and Dumplings

Bonnie Miller, Louisville, OH

Makes 4 servings
Prep. Time: 10 minutes ⚬ *Cook Time: 3 minutes*

1 Tbsp. olive oil

1 small onion, chopped

2 celery ribs, cut into 1-inch pieces

6 small carrots, cut into 1-inch chunks

2 cups chicken broth

2 lb. boneless, skinless chicken breast halves, cut into 1-inch pieces

2 chicken bouillon cubes

1 tsp. salt

1 tsp. pepper

1 tsp. poultry seasoning

Biscuits:

2 cups buttermilk biscuit mix

½ cup plus 1 Tbsp. milk

1 tsp. parsley

1. Set the Instant Pot to the Sauté function and heat the olive oil.

2. Add the onion, celery, and carrots to the hot oil and sauté for 3 to 5 minutes.

3. Pour in the broth and scrape the bottom of the inner pot with a wooden spoon or spatula to deglaze. Press Cancel.

4. Add the chicken, bouillon, salt, pepper, and poultry seasoning.

5. Combine the biscuit ingredients in a bowl until just moistened. Drop 2-tablespoon mounds over the contents of the inner pot, as evenly spaced out as possible.

6. Secure the lid and set the vent to sealing. Manually set the cook time for 3 minutes.

7. When the cook time is over, manually release the pressure.

Crustless Chicken Potpie

Hope Comerford, Clinton Township, MI

Makes 6 servings
Prep. Time: 15 minutes ⚘ Cook Time: 30 minutes

1 lb. boneless, skinless chicken breasts

3 Yukon Gold potatoes, peeled and chopped into ½-inch cubes

1 cup chopped onion

2 carrots, chopped

¾ cup frozen peas

¾ cup frozen corn

½ cup chopped celery

10¾-oz. can condensed cream of chicken soup

1 cup milk

1 cup chicken broth

1 tsp. salt

1 tsp. garlic powder

1 tsp. onion powder

2 Tbsp. cornstarch

2 Tbsp. cold water

16.3-oz. can flaky biscuits

1. Place all of the ingredients, except for the cornstarch, water, and biscuits, into the inner pot of the Instant Pot.

2. Secure the lid and set the vent to sealing. Manually set the cook time for 25 minutes on high pressure.

3. While the Instant Pot is cooking, bake the canned biscuits according to the directions on the can.

4. When the cook time is over, manually release the pressure.

5. When the pin drops, remove the lid. Remove the chicken to a bowl. Press Cancel then press Sauté.

6. Mix together the cornstarch and water. Stir this into the contents of the Instant Pot and cook until thickened, about 5 minutes. Meanwhile, shred the chicken, then add it back in with the contents of the inner pot.

7. Serve with the freshly baked flaky biscuits.

Hot Chicken Sandwiches

Hope Comerford, Clinton Township, MI

Makes 12 servings
Prep. Time: 5 minutes & Cook Time: 12 minutes

4 boneless, skinless chicken breasts

2 cups chicken broth

10¾-oz. can condensed cream of chicken soup

1 tsp. garlic powder

1 tsp. onion powder

¼ tsp. pepper

1½ cups crushed wavy potato chips, Ritz crackers, or saltines

12 hamburger buns

1. Place the chicken breasts in the inner pot of the Instant Pot.

2. Mix together the chicken broth with cream of chicken soup, garlic powder, onion powder, and pepper. Pour it over the chicken.

3. Secure the lid and set the vent to sealing. Manually set the cook time for 12 minutes on high pressure.

4. When the cook time is over, let the pressure release naturally.

5. When the pin drops, remove the lid. Remove the chicken to a bowl and shred it between 2 forks. Stir it back through the sauce in the inner pot along with the crushed chips.

6. Serve on hamburger buns.

Serving suggestion:

These are delicious with pickles added to each sandwich.

Chicken Enchilada Casserole

Hope Comerford, Clinton Township, MI

Makes 4–6 servings
Prep. Time: 20 minutes ⚕ *Cook Time: 33 minutes*

1½ lb. boneless, skinless chicken breasts

1 cup chicken broth

2 cups red enchilada sauce, *divided*

4-oz. can diced green chilies

½ cup diced onion

1 tsp. salt

1 tsp. cumin

1 tsp. chili powder

1 tsp. garlic powder

½ tsp. onion powder

⅛ tsp. pepper

Nonstick cooking spray

10 soft corn tortillas

1½ cups shredded Mexican-blend cheese

1 cup water

1. Place the chicken breasts in the inner pot of the Instant Pot along with the chicken broth and ¼ cup of the red enchilada sauce.

2. Secure the lid and set the vent to sealing. Manually set the cook time for 15 minutes.

3. When the cook time is over, let the pressure release naturally for 10 minutes, then manually release the remaining pressure.

4. Remove the chicken and shred between 2 forks in a medium bowl. Discard the liquid from the inner pot and wipe clean.

5. To the shredded chicken, add the green chilies, onion, salt, cumin, chili powder, garlic powder, onion powder, and pepper. Stir.

6. Spray a 7-inch round baking pan with nonstick cooking spray.

7. Pour in ¼ cup of the enchilada sauce and coat the bottom. Layer in approximately 3 tortillas (cut if necessary), half of the chicken, ½ cup of shredded cheese, and ¾ cup of enchilada sauce. Repeat this process again. Top the casserole with the remaining tortillas, enchilada sauce, and cheese. Cover with foil.

8. Pour 1 cup of water into the inner pot of the Instant Pot. Place the trivet on top with handles up. Carefully place the baking pan on top of the trivet.

9. Secure the lid and set the vent to sealing. Manually set the cook time for 18 minutes.

10. When the cook time is over, manually release the pressure. Remove the casserole carefully and let it sit uncovered for about 5 minutes before digging in.

Traditional Turkey Breast

Hope Comerford, Clinton Township, MI

Makes 6 servings
Prep. Time: 10 minutes & Cook Time: 35 minutes

7-lb. or less turkey breast

2 cups turkey broth

1–2 Tbsp. olive oil

Rub:

2 tsp. garlic powder

1 tsp. onion powder

1 tsp. salt

¼ tsp. pepper

1 tsp. poultry seasoning

1. Remove the gizzards from the turkey breast, rinse it, and pat it dry.

2. Place the trivet into the inner pot of the Instant Pot, then pour in the broth.

3. Mix together the rub ingredients in a small bowl.

4. Rub the turkey all over with olive oil, then press the rub onto the turkey breast all over.

5. Place the turkey breast onto the trivet, breast-side up.

6. Secure the lid and set the vent to sealing. Manually set the cook time for 35 minutes on high pressure.

7. When the cook time is over, let the pressure release naturally.

Tip:

If you want the breast to have crispy skin, remove it from the Instant Pot and place it under the broiler in the oven for a few minutes, or until skin is as crispy as you like it.

Turkey Thighs, Acorn Squash, and Apples

Mary E. Wheatley, Mashpee, MA

Makes 6–8 servings
Prep. Time: 10 minutes ☙ Cook Time: 35 minutes

1 tsp. olive oil

1 shallot, or small onion, chopped

4 turkey thighs, skin and excess fat removed

Salt and pepper to taste

1 cup apple juice, or cider

2-lb. acorn squash, peeled, seeded, and cut into 1-inch-thick rings

6 Granny Smith, or other tart, apples cored and cut into ½-inch-thick rings

1 Tbsp. apple brandy

3 Tbsp. brown sugar

1 tsp. ground cinnamon

½ tsp. ground allspice

1. Set the Instant Pot to the Sauté function and heat up the olive oil.

2. When the oil is hot, add the shallot to the inner pot and sauté for about 2 minutes.

3. Sprinkle the turkey thighs with the salt and pepper, then sear the turkey thighs on both sides. (This should only take a few more minutes.) Remove them onto a plate and set aside for a moment.

4. Pour the apple juice into the inner pot and deglaze the bottom of the pot by scraping with a wooden spoon or spatula. Press Cancel.

5. Arrange the turkey thighs back in the inner pot, with the squash and apple rings on top.

6. In a small bowl, combine the brandy, brown sugar, cinnamon, and allspice. Pour over the squash, apples, and turkey.

7. Secure the lid and set the vent to sealing. Manually set the cook time for 30 minutes on high pressure.

8. When the cook time is over, let the pressure release naturally.

Turkey Tetrazzini

Hope Comerford, Clinton Township, MI

Makes 6–8 servings
Prep. Time: 10 minutes ⚬ Cook Time: 3 minutes

2 Tbsp. butter

I cup chopped onion

I cup sliced mushrooms

3 cups chicken broth, *divided*

12 oz. wide egg noodles

2 cups chopped leftover turkey

I cup frozen peas

½ tsp. salt

⅛ tsp. pepper

I cup half-and-half

1½ cups shredded mozzarella cheese

½ cup grated or shredded Parmesan cheese

1. Set the Instant Pot to the Sauté function. Add the butter.

2. Sauté the onion and mushrooms in the melted butter for 2 to 3 minutes.

3. Pour in 1 cup of the chicken broth and scrape the bottom of the pot with a wooden spoon or spatula. Press Cancel.

4. Evenly spread the egg noodles around the Instant Pot, not stirring. Just press. Layer the turkey and peas over the top of the noodles and sprinkle with salt and pepper. Pour the remaining 2 cups of broth over the top.

5. Secure the lid and set the vent to sealing. Manually set the cook time for 3 minutes.

6. When the cook time is over, manually release the pressure.

7. When the pin drops, remove the lid and add the half-and-half and cheese, then stir together.

8. Let it sit for a bit to thicken, then serve.

Brown Sugar and Honey Ham

Hope Comerford, Clinton Township, MI

Makes 13–15 servings
Prep. Time: 5 minutes ⚜ *Cook Time: 11–18 minutes*

1 cup orange juice
1 cup brown sugar
½ tsp. ground cloves
3–5-lb. spiral ham
2 Tbsp. honey

1. Place the trivet, handles up, into the inner pot of the Instant Pot. Pour in the orange juice.

2. In a small bowl, mix together the brown sugar and cloves.

3. Place the ham on top of the trivet, then pour the honey on top of the ham, coating it. Press half of the brown sugar and clove mixture onto the ham as best you can. (If the fit is tight, perhaps do this step on top of a cutting board, then lower the ham onto the trivet.)

4. Secure the lid and set the vent to sealing. Set the cook time manually for 6 minutes for a 3-lb. ham, 8 minutes for a 4-lb. ham, or 10 minutes for a 5-lb. ham.

5. When the cook time is over, manually release the pressure. Press Cancel.

6. Remove the trivet with the ham and set aside.

7. Set the Instant Pot to Sauté and pour in the remaining brown sugar and clove mixture. Cook for about 5 to 8 minutes, allowing the liquid to reduce. Stir frequently so the glaze does not burn.

8. Pour the glaze from the inner pot over the ham and between the slices. Serve and enjoy!

Autumn Harvest Pork Loin

Stacy Schmucker Stoltzfus, Enola, PA

Makes 4–6 servings
Prep. Time: 10 minutes   ♣   Cook Time: 30 minutes

1 Tbsp. olive oil
1½–2-lb. pork loin
Salt
Pepper
1 cup cider or apple juice
2 large Granny Smith apples, peeled and sliced
1½ whole butternut squash, peeled and cubed
½ cup brown sugar
¼ tsp. cinnamon
¼ tsp. dried thyme
¼ tsp. dried sage

1. Set the Instant Pot to the Sauté function. Heat the olive oil.

2. Sprinkle the loin with salt and pepper on all sides. Sear the loin on all sides in the hot oil.

3. Remove the loin and set aside. Pour in the cider or juice and deglaze the bottom of the inner pot by scraping with a wooden spatula or spoon. Press Cancel.

4. Place the loin back into the inner pot.

5. In a large bowl, combine the apples and squash. Sprinkle with the brown sugar, cinnamon, thyme, and sage. Stir. Spoon around pork loin in inner pot.

6. Secure the lid and set the vent to sealing. Manually set the cook time for 30 minutes on high pressure.

7. When the cook time is over, let the pressure release naturally.

8. Remove the pork from the Instant Pot. Let stand 10–15 minutes. Slice into ½-inch-thick slices.

9. Serve topped with the apples and squash.

Cranberry-Apple Stuffed Pork Loin

Hope Comerford, Clinton Township, MI

Makes 4–6 servings
Prep. Time: 20 minutes 🌿 Cook Time: 30 minutes

3-lb. pork tenderloin

2 Tbsp. Dijon mustard

1 Tbsp. brown sugar

1 cup diced apple (skins removed)

½ cup dried cranberries

1½ tsp. sea salt, *divided*

¼ tsp. pepper, *divided*

1 tsp. garlic powder

1 tsp. onion powder

½ tsp. dried rosemary

¼ tsp. dried sage

3 Tbsp. olive oil, *divided*

2 medium onions, peeled and chopped into thick segments

1 cup chicken broth

1. Butterfly the tenderloin and pound it so that it is evenly thick across.

2. In a small bowl, mix the Dijon mustard and brown sugar. Spread this over the tenderloin.

3. In another bowl, mix the diced apple and cranberries with ¼ teaspoon of sea salt and ⅛ teaspoon of pepper. Spread it over the tenderloin, staying about ½ inch from the edges.

4. Roll the tenderloin as tightly as possible and tie in several places with cooking twine.

5. Mix the remaining sea salt, the garlic powder, the onion powder, the rosemary, the sage, and the remaining pepper and pat it onto the tenderloin, covering it on all sides.

6. Set the Instant Pot to the Sauté function and pour in 1½ tablespoons olive oil to heat.

7. When the oil is hot, carefully sear the tenderloin on all sides. This will take 5 to 10 minutes. Remove the pork loin and set aside.

8. Pour in the remaining olive oil and add the onions. Cook for about 4 minutes, or until slightly translucent.

9. Pour in the broth and scrape the bottom of the pot with a wooden spoon or spatula to deglaze. Press Cancel.

10. Place the tenderloin on top of the onions.

11. Secure the lid and set the vent to sealing. Set the cook time for 30 minutes on the Meat setting.

12. When the cook time is over, let the pressure release naturally.

Holiday Pork Chops

Hope Comerford, Clinton Township, MI

Makes 6 servings
Prep. Time: 5 minutes ⚶ Cook Time: 8 minutes

6 boneless pork chops, 1 inch to
1½ inches thick

14-oz. can whole cranberry sauce

½ cup apple juice

¼ cup chicken broth

2 Tbsp. Liquid Aminos

1 Tbsp. dried minced onion

1 tsp. garlic powder

¼ tsp. pepper

1. Arrange the pork chops in the inner pot of the Instant Pot.

2. Mix the remaining ingredients in a bowl and pour over the chops.

3. Secure the lid and set the vent to sealing. Manually set the cook time for 8 minutes on high pressure.

4. When the cook time is over, let the pressure release naturally for 10 minutes, then manually release the remaining pressure.

Tender Tasty Ribs

Carol Eveleth, Cheyenne, WY

Makes 2–3 servings
Prep. Time: 5 minutes   ♣   Cook Time: 35 minutes

2 tsp. salt

2 tsp. black pepper

I tsp. garlic powder

I tsp. onion powder

I slab baby back ribs

I cup water

I cup barbecue sauce, *divided*

1. Mix the salt, pepper, garlic powder, and onion powder together. Rub seasoning mixture on both sides of slab of ribs. Cut slab in half if it's too big for the Instant Pot.

2. Pour the water into the inner pot of the Instant Pot. Place the ribs into pot, drizzle with ¼ cup of sauce, and secure the lid. Make sure the vent is set to sealing.

3. Set it to Manual for 25 minutes. It will take a few minutes to heat up and seal the vent. When the cook time is over, let it sit 5 minutes, then release steam by turning valve to venting. Turn oven on to broil (or heat the grill) while you're waiting for the 5-minute resting time.

4. Remove ribs from Instant Pot and place on a baking sheet. Slather both sides with remaining ¾ cup sauce.

5. Place under broiler (or on grill) for 5–10 minutes, watching carefully so it doesn't burn. Remove and brush with a bit more sauce. Pull apart and dig in!

Prime Rib

Hope Comerford, Clinton Township, MI

Makes 6 servings
Prep. Time: 2 to 3 hours and 40 minutes   ⚶   Refrigeration Time: 24 hours
Cook Time: 45 minutes   ⚶   Rest Time: 15 minutes

3–4-lb. boneless prime rib roast

2 Tbsp. pink sea salt

2 Tbsp. garlic powder

1 ½ Tbsp. pepper

½ lb. butter, room temperature

1 cup beef stock

½ cup red wine

2 Tbsp. olive oil

3 Tbsp. cornstarch

3 Tbsp. cold water

1. Score the layer of fat on the rib roast with slits 1 inch apart in a crisscross pattern.

2. Mix the sea salt, garlic powder, and pepper. Rub this all over the prime rib, including into the slits.

3. Refrigerate the roast, uncovered, for at least 24 hours.

4. When you're ready to cook the prime rib, remove it from the refrigerator and let it sit for 2 to 3 hours. When the 2 to 3 hours is up, rub it all over with the butter.

5. Pour the beef stock and red wine into the inner pot of the Instant Pot and place the trivet on top. Place the prime rib on top of the trivet.

6. Secure the lid and set the vent to sealing. Manually set the cook time for 5 minutes.

7. When the cook time is over, do not release the pressure or remove the lid. Let it sit for 30 minutes.

8. After 30 minutes, remove the lid and check the meat temperature with a meat thermometer. You will want it to be around 115°F. If it's not there yet, put the cover back on and let it sit for 5 to 10 more minutes and check again.

9. Remove the prime rib and set it aside. Remove the trivet. Pour the contents of the inner pot into a bowl and set aside.

(Continued on next page)

10. Set the Instant Pot to the Sauté function. Heat up the olive oil. Once the oil is heated, sear the roast on all sides. This will take 10 to 15 minutes. Check the temperature. For a medium- rare roast, you will want it to be 135°F. Place the prime rib on a cutting board or plate and tent with foil. Let is rest about 15 minutes.

11. To make gravy from the liquid you set aside, pour the liquid back into the inner pot. Mix together the cornstarch and water, then mix into the liquid in the inner pot. Cook until thickened to your liking, or about 5 to 10 minutes.

Mississippi Pot Roast

Hope Comerford, Clinton Township, MI

Makes 8 servings
Prep. Time: 10–12 minutes ☙ Cook Time: 60 minutes

2 Tbsp. olive oil

3–4-lb. chuck roast (cut into large chunks to fit the Instant Pot if necessary)

½ cup beef broth

1-oz. pkg. dry ranch seasoning

1-oz. pkg. au jus gravy mix

16-oz. jar sliced peperoncini, with juice

Serving suggestion:

This is also delicious served on sub rolls with melted cheese on top, or open-faced sandwiches.

1. Set the Instant Pot to the Sauté setting and heat the olive oil. Sear the chuck roast on all sides. This will take 8 to 10 minutes.

2. Remove the roast and set aside. Pour in the beef broth and scrape the bottom of the inner pot with a wooden spoon or spatula to scrape up any bits. Press Cancel.

3. Place the roast back in the inner pot and sprinkle with the ranch seasoning and au jus gravy mix. Pour the jar of peperoncini over the top, including the juices.

4. Secure the lid and set the vent to sealing. Manually set the cook time for 60 minutes on high pressure.

5. When the cook time is over, let the pressure release naturally for 15 minutes, then manually release the remaining pressure.

6. When the pin drops, remove the roast and shred between 2 forks. Discard any large pieces of fat.

7. Skim off as much fat from the juice in the inner pot as possible, then stir the shredded roast back through.

8. Serve over mashed potatoes.

Tip:

If you are pressed for time, you can skip the sauté step, but it is highly recommended.

Braised Beef with Cranberries

Audrey L. Kneer, Williamsfield, IL

Makes 8 servings
Prep. Time: 20 minutes ⚜ *Cook Time: 60 minutes*

2 lb. sliced, well-trimmed top round beef

⅛ tsp. pepper

1 Tbsp. olive oil

1 medium onion, chopped

2 cloves garlic, chopped

½ cup peeled and diced turnip

1 medium carrot, chopped

1 rib celery, cut fine

1 cup low-sugar apple juice

1 cup fresh, or frozen (thawed), cranberries

1 sprig parsley

1 bay leaf

1. Rub the beef with the pepper. Set aside.

2. Set the Instant Pot to Sauté and heat the olive oil in the inner pot.

3. Sauté the beef for about 10 minutes, searing each side.

4. Remove the beef and set it aside.

5. Sauté the onion and garlic for about 3 minutes, then add the turnip, carrot, and celery and continue sautéing for about 5 more minutes.

6. Pour in the apple juice and scrape the bottom of the pot to deglaze.

7. Press Cancel. Add the beef back in, as well as the cranberries, parsley, and bay leaf. Make sure the sprig of parsley and bay leaf are tucked into the liquid.

8. Secure the lid and set the vent to sealing.

9. Set the cook time manually for 60 minutes on high pressure.

10. When the cook time is over, let the pressure release naturally for 10 minutes, then manually release the remaining pressure.

Beef Burgundy

Jacqueline Stefl, East Bethany, NY

Makes 6 servings
Prep. Time: 30 minutes ⚜ Cook Time: 30 minutes

2 Tbsp. olive oil

2 lb. stewing meat, cubed, trimmed of fat

2½ Tbsp. flour

5 medium onions, thinly sliced

½ lb. fresh mushrooms, sliced

1 tsp. salt

¼ tsp. dried marjoram

¼ tsp. dried thyme

⅛ tsp. pepper

¾ cup beef broth

1½ cups burgundy

1. Press Sauté on the Instant Pot and add the olive oil.

2. Dredge the meat in the flour, then brown in batches in the Instant Pot. Set aside the meat. Sauté the onions and mushrooms in the remaining oil and drippings for about 3–4 minutes, then add the meat back in. Press Cancel.

3. Add the salt, marjoram, thyme, pepper, broth, and wine to the Instant Pot.

4. Secure the lid and make sure the vent is set to sealing. Press the Manual button and set to 30 minutes.

5. When the cook time is over, let the pressure release naturally for 15 minutes, then perform a quick release.

6. Serve over cooked noodles.

Barbecued Brisket

Dorothy Dyer, Lee's Summit, MO

Makes 9–12 servings
Prep. Time: 10 minutes ♣ Cook Time: 70 minutes

1 cup beef broth
⅓ cup Italian salad dressing
1½ tsp. liquid smoke
⅓ cup + 2 tsp. brown sugar, packed
½ tsp. celery salt
½ tsp. salt
1 Tbsp. Worcestershire sauce
½ tsp. black pepper
¼ tsp. chili powder
½ tsp. garlic powder
3–4-lb. beef brisket
1¼ cups barbecue sauce
Sandwich rolls

1. Pour the beef broth, Italian dressing, liquid smoke, brown sugar, celery salt, salt, Worcestershire sauce, pepper, chili powder, and garlic powder into the inner pot of the Instant Pot. Stir. Place the brisket into the broth mixture. You may cut it into pieces if needed for it to fit under the broth.

2. Secure the lid and set the vent to sealing. Manually set the cook time for 70 minutes on high pressure.

3. When the cook time is over, let the pressure release naturally.

4. Lift the meat out of the Instant Pot and shred it in a bowl. Pour the barbecue sauce over the meat and stir. Serve on sandwich rolls.

Cranberry Brisket

Roseann Wilson, Albuquerque, NM

Makes 5–6 servings
Prep. Time: 5 minutes ⚓ Cook Time: 70 minutes

1 cup beef broth

16-oz. can whole-berry cranberry sauce

8-oz. can tomato sauce

½ cup chopped onions

1 Tbsp. prepared mustard

2½-lb. beef brisket

½ tsp. salt

¼ tsp. pepper

1. Combine the beef broth, cranberry sauce, tomato sauce, onions, and mustard in the inner pot of the Instant Pot.

2. Rub the brisket with salt and pepper. Place into the sauce in the inner pot.

3. Secure the lid and set the vent to sealing. Manually set the cook time for 70 minutes.

4. When the cook time is over, let the pressure release naturally.

5. When the pin drops, remove the lid, then remove the brisket. Slice thinly across the grain. Skim the fat from the juices. Serve the juices with the brisket.

Pot Roast

Carol Eveleth, Cheyenne, WY

Makes 4 servings
Prep. Time: 20 minutes & Cook Time: 103 minutes

2-lb. beef roast, boneless

¼ tsp. salt, and more to taste

¼ tsp. pepper, and more to taste

1 Tbsp. olive oil

2 stalks celery, chopped

4 Tbsp. butter

2 cups tomato juice

2 cloves garlic, finely chopped, or 1 tsp. garlic powder

1 tsp. thyme

1 bay leaf

4 carrots, chopped

1 medium onion, chopped

4 medium potatoes, chopped

1. Pat the beef dry with paper towels; season on all sides with ¼ teaspoon each of the salt and pepper.

2. Select Sauté function on the Instant Pot and adjust heat to more. Put the oil in the inner pot, then cook the beef in oil for 6 minutes, until browned, turning once. Set on plate.

3. Add the celery and butter to the inner pot; cook 2 minutes. Stir in the tomato juice, garlic, thyme, and bay leaf. Hit Cancel to turn off Sauté function.

4. Place the beef on top of the contents of the inner pot and press it into the sauce. Cover and lock lid and make sure the vent is on sealing. Select Manual and cook at high pressure for 75 minutes.

5. Once cooking is complete, release pressure by using natural release function. Transfer the beef to a cutting board. Discard the bay leaf.

6. Skim off any excess fat from surface. Choose Sauté function and adjust heat to More. Cook 18 minutes, or until reduced by about half (2 cups). Hit Cancel to turn off Sauté function.

7. Add the carrots, onion, and potatoes. Cover and lock lid and make sure the vent is on sealing. Select Manual and cook at high pressure for 10 minutes.

8. Once cooking is complete, release pressure by using a quick release. Using Sauté function, keep at a simmer.

9. Season with more salt and pepper to taste.

Instant Pot Boneless Short Ribs

Hope Comerford, Clinton Township, MI

Makes 4 servings
Prep. Time: 20 minutes & Cook Time: 53–55 minutes

1 ½ Tbsp. olive oil

3 lb. boneless short ribs

½ tsp. salt

⅛ tsp. pepper

1 large onion, sliced

6 cloves garlic, smashed

1 cup beef stock

¼ cup balsamic vinegar

¾ cup red wine

4 carrots, cut into 2-inch chunks

Sprig rosemary

Sprig thyme

2 Tbsp. cold water

2 Tbsp. cornstarch

Serving suggestion:
Serve with mashed or baked potatoes.

1. Set the Instant Pot to the Sauté function and pour in the olive oil.

2. Sprinkle the short ribs with the salt and pepper, then brown them on all sides in the inner pot. Do this in batches if necessary. Set them aside.

3. Add the onion and garlic to the inner pot and sauté for 3 to 5 minutes.

4. Pour the beef stock into the inner pot and scrape the bottom to remove any bits that may be stuck. Press Cancel.

5. Place the short ribs back into the inner pot, along with the balsamic vinegar, red wine, carrots, rosemary, and thyme.

6. Secure the lid and set the vent to sealing. Manually set the cook time for 50 minutes on high pressure.

7. When the cook time is over, let the pressure release naturally for 20 minutes, then release the remaining pressure manually.

8. Switch the Instant Pot to the Sauté function.

9. Mix the cold water and cornstarch. Gently stir this mixture into the contents of the inner pot and let simmer until the sauce is thickened a bit, about 3 to 5 minutes.

10. Serve the short ribs and carrots with the sauce spooned over the top.

Stuffed Cabbage

Hope Comerford, Clinton Township, MI

Makes 12–15 stuffed cabbage rolls
Prep. Time: 30 minutes   &   Cook Time: 20 minutes

12 cups water

1 large head cabbage (you will use about 12–15 leaves)

1 lb. 95%-fat-free ground beef

1 medium onion, chopped

2 cloves garlic, chopped

1 tsp. chopped fresh parsley

¼ tsp. salt

½ tsp. pepper

1 egg, beaten

¾ cup brown rice, uncooked

1 cup water

1 Tbsp. vinegar

16 oz. low-sugar, low-sodium marinara sauce, *divided*

2 tsp. Italian seasoning

1. Pour the water into the inner pot and press Sauté on the Instant Pot. Bring the water to a boil.

2. Gently lower the cabbage into the water and cook for about 5 minutes, turning to be sure all the outer leaves are softened. Press Cancel.

3. Remove the cabbage and carefully drain the water. Peel off 12 to 15 leaves.

4. In a bowl, mix together the beef, onion, garlic, parsley, salt, pepper, egg, and brown rice with a wooden spoon or clean hands.

5. On a clean surface, lay out the cabbage leaves. (You may need to thin some of the thicker ribs of the cabbage leaves with a paring knife.) Evenly divide the filling among the leaves. Roll them burrito style, tucking in the ends and rolling tightly. If you need to, you can use a toothpick to hold them closed.

6. Pour the water and vinegar into the inner pot. Gently place the cabbage rolls into the pot, pouring a little sauce on top of each layer and finishing with a layer of sauce. Sprinkle with the Italian seasoning.

7. Secure the lid and set the vent to sealing.

8. Set the Instant Pot to cook manually for 20 minutes on high pressure.

9. When the cook time is over, let the pressure release naturally for 20 minutes and then manually release the remaining pressure.

10. When the pin drops, remove the lid. Serve hot.

Steak Stroganoff

Hope Comerford, Clinton Township, MI

Makes 6 servings
Prep. Time: 35 minutes ♣ Cook Time: 15 minutes

3–4 Tbsp. olive oil

½ cup flour

½ tsp. garlic powder

½ tsp. onion powder

½ tsp. salt

⅛ tsp. pepper

2-lb. boneless beef chuck roast, trimmed of fat, cut into 1½ × ½-inch strips.

9 oz. sliced mushrooms

½ cup chopped red onion

1 cup beef stock

10¾-oz. can condensed cream of mushroom soup

⅓ cup Liquid Aminos or soy sauce

½ cup fat-free sour cream

6 servings of cooked egg noodles, elbow noodles, or brown rice ramen noodles

1. Place the oil in the Instant Pot and press Sauté.

2. Combine the flour, garlic powder, onion powder, salt, and pepper in a medium bowl. Stir the beef pieces through the flour mixture until they are evenly coated.

3. Lightly brown the steak pieces in the oil in the Instant Pot, about 2 minutes each side. Let them drain and cool on a paper towel. Do this in batches, adding more oil to the pot with each batch if needed. Set them aside.

4. Pour the mushrooms and red onion into the inner pot and sauté for about 5 minutes.

5. Pour the stock into the inner pot and scrape the bottom vigorously. This will prevent you from getting a burn notice when the Instant Pot pressurizes.

6. Stir in the cream of mushroom soup and Liquid Aminos.

7. Secure the lid and set the vent to sealing. Manually set the cook time for 10 minutes on high pressure.

8. When the cook time is over, let the pressure release naturally for 10 minutes, then release the rest manually.

9. Remove the lid and switch the Instant Pot to the Sauté function. Stir in the sour cream. Let the sauce come to a boil and cook for about 5 minutes.

10. Serve over the cooked noodles.

Beef Goulash

Colleen Heatwole, Burton, MI

Makes 6 servings
Prep. Time: 15 minutes ⚜ *Cook Time: 50 minutes*

2 lb. beef stew meat cut into 2-inch pieces

I large onion, chopped

3 carrots, cut into 2-inch chunks

I medium red bell pepper, chopped

I cup beef broth

¼ cup ketchup

2 tsp. Worcestershire sauce

2 tsp. paprika

2 tsp. minced garlic

I tsp. salt

1. Place all the ingredients into the inner pot of the Instant Pot.

2. Secure the lid and set the vent to sealing. Manually set the cook time for 50 minutes on high pressure.

3. When the cook time is over, let the pressure release naturally for 20 minutes, then manually release the remaining pressure.

Serving suggestion:

Mashed potatoes and green beans go well as sides, or serve with cooked barley or rice.

Christmas Meat Loaf

Wafi Brandt, Manheim, PA

Makes 4–6 servings
Prep. Time: 10 minutes ⚶ *Cook Time: 25 minutes*

1 cup water
Nonstick cooking spray

Meat Loaf:
2 eggs
1 envelope dry onion soup mix
½ cup seasoned bread crumbs
¼ cup chopped dried cranberries
1 tsp. parsley
1½ lb. ground beef

Sauce:
8-oz. can whole-berry cranberry sauce
½ cup ketchup
2 Tbsp. brown sugar
3 Tbsp. finely chopped onions
2 tsp. cider vinegar

1. Set the trivet inside the inner pot of the Instant Pot and pour in the water.

2. Spray a 7-inch springform or round baking pan with nonstick cooking spray. Mix all meat loaf ingredients together in a large bowl. Shape into the springform pan.

3. Blend together the sauce ingredients in a small bowl. Spread mixture on top of meat. Cover the pan with aluminum foil.

4. Place the springform pan on top of the trivet inside the inner pot. Secure the lid and set the vent to sealing.

5. Manually set the cook time for 25 minutes on high pressure.

6. When the cook time is over, let the pressure release naturally for 10 minutes, then manually release the remaining pressure.

7. Remove the lid and use oven mitts to carefully remove the trivet from the inner pot.

8. Allow the meat loaf to stand 10 minutes before slicing to serve.

Cottage Pie

Hope Comerford, Clinton Township, MI

Makes 4–6 servings
Prep. Time: 20 minutes ⚖ *Cook Time: 18 minutes*

3 Yukon Gold potatoes, peeled and cut into 1-inch cubes

1 tsp. salt

2 cups water, *divided*

2–3 carrots, peeled and cut in half

½ cup milk

¼ cup butter

1 cup shredded cheddar cheese

1 lb. ground beef

½ cup chopped onion

1 cup frozen peas

2 tsp. Worcestershire sauce

¼ tsp. pepper

1 cup beef broth

2 Tbsp. cornstarch

Nonstick cooking spray

1. Place the potatoes, salt, and 1 cup of the water into the inner pot of the Instant Pot. Place a steamer basket or rack on top with the carrots.

2. Secure the lid and set the vent to sealing. Manually set the cook time for 8 minutes.

3. When the cook time is over, manually release the pressure. Press Cancel.

4. Carefully remove the steamer basket or rack and set the carrots aside to cool a bit. Drain the potatoes, then transfer them to a mixing bowl. Wipe out the inner pot.

5. Mash the potatoes, milk, butter, and cheddar with a potato masher or hand mixer. Set aside.

6. Set the Instant Pot to the Sauté function and brown the beef with the onion. Once cooked, remove the beef/onion mixture and set aside in a medium bowl. Press Cancel. Wipe out the inner pot.

7. Chop the carrots you cooked earlier. Place them in the bowl with the beef, along with the frozen peas.

8. Mix the beef/vegetable mixture with the Worcestershire sauce, pepper, beef broth, and cornstarch.

9. Spray a 1½-quart round baking dish that fits in the inner pot with nonstick cooking spray. Pour the beef/vegetable mixture in and top with the mashed potatoes. Cover with foil.

(Continued on next page)

10. Pour the other cup of water into the inner pot and place the trivet with handles up on top. Carefully place the baking dish on top.

11. Secure the lid and set the vent to sealing. Manually set the cook time for 10 minutes on high pressure.

12. When the cook time is over, manually release the pressure.

13. When the pin drops, remove the lid, then carefully remove the baking dish from the inner pot with hot pads. Serve and enjoy!

Sloppy Joes

Hope Comerford, Clinton Township, MI

Makes 8–10 servings
Prep. Time: 8–10 minutes   ⚷   Cook Time: 5 minutes

1 Tbsp. olive oil

1 cup chopped red onion

½ green bell pepper, chopped

½ red bell pepper, chopped

1 lb. lean ground beef

1 lb. bulk mild pork sausage

½ cup water

8-oz. can tomato sauce

½ cup ketchup

¼ cup tightly packed brown sugar

2 Tbsp. apple cider vinegar

2 Tbsp. yellow mustard

1 Tbsp. Worcestershire sauce

1 Tbsp. chili powder

1 tsp. garlic powder

1 tsp. onion powder

¼ tsp. salt

¼ tsp. pepper

1. Set the Instant Pot to the Sauté function and add the olive oil.

2. When the oil is heated, sauté the red onion and bell peppers for about 3 minutes.

3. Add the ground beef and pork sausage. Brown until no longer pink, for about 5 to 7 minutes. (Drain the grease if necessary.)

4. Add the water and scrape the bottom of the inner pot with a wooden spoon or spatula, scraping up any stuck on bits.

5. Add the remaining ingredients. Stir.

6. Secure the lid and set the vent to sealing. Manually set the cook time for 5 minutes on high pressure.

7. When the cook time is over, let the pressure release naturally for 10 minutes, then manually release the remaining pressure.

8. Serve on hamburger buns.

Lasagna the Instant Pot Way

Hope Comerford, Clinton Township, MI

Makes 8 servings
Prep. Time: 15 minutes ⚬ Cook Time: 15 minutes

1 Tbsp. olive oil

1 lb. extra-lean ground beef or ground turkey

½ cup chopped onion ½ tsp. salt

⅛ tsp. pepper

2 cups water

12 lasagna noodles

8 oz. cottage cheese

1 egg

1 tsp. Italian seasoning

4 cups spinach, chopped or torn

1 cup sliced mushrooms

28 oz. marinara sauce

1 cup mozzarella cheese

1. Set the Instant Pot to the Sauté function and heat the olive oil. Brown the beef and onion with the salt and pepper. This will take about 5 minutes. Because you're using extra-lean ground beef, there should not be much grease, but if so, you'll need to drain it before continuing. Remove half of the ground beef and set aside. Press Cancel.

2. Pour in the water.

3. Break 4 noodles in half and arrange them on top of the beef and water.

4. Mix together the cottage cheese, egg, and Italian seasoning until the mixture is smooth. Smooth half of this mixture over the lasagna noodles.

5. Layer half of the spinach and half of the mushrooms on top.

6. Break 4 more noodles in half and lay them on top of what you just did. Spread out the remaining cottage cheese mixture.

7. Layer on the remaining spinach and mushrooms, then pour half of the marinara sauce over the top.

8. Finish with breaking the remaining 4 noodles in half and laying them on top of the previous layer. Spread the remaining marinara sauce on top.

9. Secure the lid and set the vent to sealing. Manually set the cook time for 7 minutes on high pressure.

10. When the cook time is over, let the pressure release naturally for 10 minutes, then manually release the remaining pressure.

11. When the pin drops, remove the lid and sprinkle the mozzarella cheese on top. Re-cover for 5 minutes.

12. When the 5 minutes is up, remove the lid. You can let this sit for a while to thicken up on "Keep Warm."

Meatless Ziti

Hope Comerford, Clinton Township, MI

Makes 8 servings
Prep. Time: 10 minutes & Cook Time: 3 minutes

1 Tbsp. olive oil

1 small onion, chopped

3 cups water, *divided*

15 oz. crushed tomatoes

8 oz. tomato sauce

1½ tsp. Italian seasoning

1 tsp. garlic powder

1 tsp. onion powder

1 tsp. sea salt

¼ tsp. pepper

12 oz. ziti

1–2 cups shredded mozzarella cheese

1. Set the Instant Pot to the Sauté function and heat the olive oil.

2. When the oil is hot, sauté the onion for 3 to 5 minutes, or until translucent.

3. Pour in 1 cup of the water and scrape any bits from the bottom of the inner pot with a wooden spoon or spatula.

4. In a bowl, mix together the crushed tomatoes, tomato sauce, Italian seasoning, garlic powder, onion powder, sea salt, and pepper. Pour 1 cup of this in the inner pot and stir.

5. Pour in the ziti. Press it down so it's in there evenly, but do not stir.

6. Pour the remaining pasta sauce evenly over the top. Again, do not stir.

7. Secure the lid and set the vent to sealing. Manually set the cook time for 3 minutes.

8. When the cook time is over, let the pressure release naturally for 10 minutes, then manually release the remaining pressure.

9. When the pin drops, remove the lid and stir in the shredded mozzarella. This will thicken as it sits a bit.

Macaroni and Cheese

Hope Comerford, Clinton Township, MI

Makes 8 servings
Prep. Time: 5 minutes & Cook Time: 4 minutes

1 lb. uncooked elbow macaroni

2 cups water

2 cups chicken broth

4 Tbsp. butter

1 tsp. salt

½ tsp. pepper

1 tsp. hot sauce

1 tsp. dried mustard

½–1 cup heavy cream or milk

1 cup shredded gouda

1 cup shredded sharp cheddar cheese

1 cup shredded Monterey Jack cheese

1. Place the macaroni, water, broth, butter, salt, pepper, hot sauce, and dried mustard into the inner pot of the Instant Pot.

2. Secure the lid and set the vent to sealing. Manually set the cook time for 4 minutes.

3. When the cook time is over, manually release the pressure.

4. When the pin drops, remove the lid and stir in the cream, starting with ½ cup. Begin stirring in the shredded cheese, 1 cup at a time. If the sauce ends up being too thin, let it sit a while and it will thicken up.

Variation:

If you want the mac and cheese to have a crust on top, pour the mac and cheese from the Instant Pot into an oven-safe baking dish. Top with additional cheese and bake in a 325°F oven for about 15 minutes.

Pumpkin Risotto

Marilyn Mowry, Irving, TX

Makes 4 servings
Prep. Time: 3 minutes ⚬ Cook Time: 6 minutes

I Tbsp. olive oil
2 onions, chopped
I garlic clove, minced
I cup raw arborio rice
I cup dry white wine
I cup low-sodium chicken broth
I cup canned pumpkin puree
¼ cup grated low-fat Parmesan cheese
Pepper to taste
⅛ tsp. ground nutmeg

1. Set the Instant Pot to the Sauté function and heat the oil in the inner pot.

2. Sauté the onions and garlic for 3 minutes.

3. Press Cancel. Stir in the rice, white wine, broth, and chicken stock. Secure the lid and set the vent to sealing.

4. Manually set the cook time for 6 minutes on high pressure.

5. When the cook time is over, manually release the pressure.

6. When the pin drops, remove the lid and stir in the pumpkin, cheese, and pepper. Let it heat through for a few minutes. Sprinkle with nutmeg. Serve at once.

Sauerbraten

Leona M. Slabaugh, Apple Creek, OH

Makes 8–10 servings
Prep. Time: 10–20 minutes   ♣   Marinating Time: 8 hours or overnight   ♣   Cook Time: 55 minutes

1 cup cider vinegar
¾ cup red wine vinegar
2 tsp. salt
½ tsp. black pepper
6 whole cloves
2 bay leaves
1 Tbsp. mustard seeds
3½-lb. boneless top round roast, tied
20 gingersnaps (about 5 oz.), crushed

1. Combine the cider vinegar, red wine vinegar, salt, pepper, cloves, bay leaves, and mustard seeds in a large bowl.

2. Place the roast in the bowl. Spoon the marinade over the roast.

3. Cover the roast with marinade and refrigerate overnight, turning once.

4. Place the roast and marinade in the inner pot of the Instant Pot.

5. Secure the lid and set the vent to sealing. Set the cook time for 55 minutes on the Meat/Stew setting.

6. When the cook time is over, let the pressure release naturally for 10 minutes, then release the remaining pressure manually.

7. When the pin drops, remove the lid, then remove roast to platter and keep warm.

8. Strain the liquid from the inner pot. Stir the crushed gingersnaps into the liquid until well blended.

9. Slice the roast and serve with the sauce alongside.

Side Dishes

Orange Honey Cranberry Sauce

Brittney Horst, Lititz, PA

Makes 6–8 servings
Prep. Time: 5 minutes ⚜ *Cook Time: 10 minutes*

3 cups fresh cranberries

½ cup orange juice (about 2 medium oranges)

½ cup 100% apple cider

1 Tbsp. orange zest

Pinch pumpkin pie spice

¼ tsp. salt

Sauté Ingredients:

¼ cup amaretto, *optional*

⅔ cup honey

1. Add the cranberries, orange juice, apple cider, orange zest, pumpkin pie spice, and salt to the inner pot of the Instant Pot. Put on the lid and set the vent to sealed. Cook on high pressure on Manual mode for 6 minutes.

2. Let the pressure release naturally.

3. Once the pressure has completely released, remove the lid, press the Cancel button to turn off the Instant Pot, then press the Sauté button and the adjust button until it sets to "less."

4. Add the sauté ingredients. Mix well with a large spoon and mash the fruit pieces as you go.

5. Cook until it reaches the thickness you desire, then turn off and store in the refrigerator once cooled.

Serving suggestion:
Great for an easy make-ahead side dish for a holiday meal!

Christmas Carrots

Lindsey Spencer, Marrow, OH

Makes 8 servings
Prep. Time: 10–15 minutes   Cook Time: 3 minutes

2 lb. carrots

½ stick (4 Tbsp.) butter, melted

½ cup water

½ cup brown sugar

8-oz. can crushed pineapple, undrained

½ cup shredded coconut

1. Peel the carrots and cut into strips ½ inch wide and 2 inches long.

2. Set the Instant Pot to the Sauté function and melt the butter.

3. Brown the carrots in the butter, about 3 to 5 minutes.

4. Pour in the water and deglaze the bottom of the inner pot with a wooden spoon or spatula. Press Cancel.

5. Add the brown sugar and pineapple to the inner pot. Mix gently.

6. Secure the lid and set the vent to sealing. Manually set the cook time for 3 minutes on high pressure.

7. When the cook time is over, manually release the pressure.

8. When the pin drops, remove the lid. Add the coconut as garnish when serving.

Green Bean Casserole

Hope Comerford, Clinton Township, MI

Makes 6 servings
Prep. Time: 5 minutes   *Cook Time: 2 minutes*

2 (14½-oz.) cans French-cut green beans, drained

⅔ cup vegetable broth

6-oz. container french-fried onions, *divided*

1 tsp. soy sauce

½ tsp. Worcestershire sauce

1 tsp. garlic powder

⅛ tsp. pepper

10¾-oz. can condensed cream of mushroom soup

¼ cup sour cream

1. Place the green beans, vegetable broth, ⅓ cup of the french-fried onions, soy sauce, Worcestershire sauce, garlic powder, and pepper into the inner pot of the Instant Pot.

2. Spread the cream of mushroom soup over the top.

3. Secure the lid and set the vent to sealing. Manually set the cook time for 2 minutes on high pressure.

4. When the cook time is over, manually release the pressure.

5. When the pin drops, remove the lid and stir in the sour cream. Once combined, pour the remaining french-fried onions over the top. Let it sit for a few minutes to thicken up.

Green Beans with Bacon

Hope Comerford, Clinton Township, MI

Makes 6 servings
Prep. Time: 7 minutes ⚬ Cook Time: 5 minutes

Nonstick cooking spray

5 slices of thick-cut bacon, chopped

½ cup chopped red onion

4 cloves garlic, chopped

¾ cups chicken stock

½ tsp. sea salt

⅛ tsp. pepper

⅛ tsp. red pepper flakes

1½ lb. fresh green beans, ends snipped and cut in half

1. Set the Instant Pot to the Sauté function and let it get nice and hot. Spray the inner pot with nonstick cooking spray and then add the bacon. Sauté until crispy.

2. Add the onion and garlic to the inner pot and sauté for an additional 2 to 3 minutes.

3. Pour in the chicken stock and scrape the bottom of the inner pot with a wooden spoon or spatula, bringing up any stuck-on bits. Press Cancel.

4. Pour in the remaining ingredients.

5. Secure the lid and set the vent to sealing. Manually set the cook time for 5 minutes on high pressure.

6. When the cook time is over, manually release the pressure.

Brussels Sprouts with Maple Glaze

Hope Comerford, Clinton Township, MI

Makes 6 servings
Prep. Time: 5–6 minutes   ☘   Cook Time: 3 minutes

4 slices thick-cut bacon, chopped

1 shallot, diced

½ cup chicken broth

1 lb. Brussels sprouts, halved if large

⅓ cup light brown sugar

1½ Tbsp. Dijon mustard

2 Tbsp. maple syrup

1. Set the Instant Pot to the Sauté function and let it get nice and hot. Spray the inner pot with nonstick cooking spray and then add the bacon. Sauté until crispy.

2. Add the shallot and sauté for 1 more minute.

3. Pour in the chicken broth and scrape the bottom of the pot with a wooden spoon or spatula. Press Cancel.

4. Pour in the Brussels sprouts and secure the lid. Set the vent to sealing.

5. Manually set the cook time for 3 minutes. When the cook time is over, manually release the pressure.

6. When the pin drops, remove the lid.

7. In a medium bowl, mix together the brown sugar, Dijon mustard, and maple syrup.

8. Remove the contents of the inner pot with a slotted spoon into the bowl with the maple glaze. Toss and serve.

Seasoned Beets

Hope Comerford, Clinton Township, MI

Makes 4–6 servings
Prep. Time: 15 minutes ⚕ Cook Time: 16 minutes

4–6 large beets, scrubbed well and tops removed

3 Tbsp. olive oil

I tsp. sea salt

¼ tsp. pepper

3 Tbsp. balsamic vinegar

I Tbsp. lemon juice

I cup water

1. Use foil to make a packet around each beet.

2. Divide the olive oil, salt, pepper, balsamic vinegar, and lemon juice evenly between each packet.

3. Pour 1 cup of water into the inner pot of the Instant Pot and place the trivet or steamer basket on top.

4. Place each beet packet onto the trivet or into the steamer basket.

5. Secure the lid and set the vent to sealing.

6. Manually set the cook time for 16 minutes on high pressure.

7. When the cook time is over, let the pressure release naturally for 10 minutes, then manually release the remaining pressure.

8. When the pin drops, remove the lid. Transfer the beets to a plate using tongs. Allow to cool and let the steam escape.

9. Once cool enough to handle, unwrap each beet packet and use a paring knife to gently peel the skin off each beet. Cut into bite-size pieces and serve with juice from the packet over the top.

Scalloped Potatoes

Hope Comerford, Clinton Township, MI

Makes 8–10 servings
Prep. Time: 15 minutes ⚬ Cook Time: 1 minute ⚬ Bake Time: 15 minutes

3 lb. white potatoes, peeled or unpeeled and sliced into 4-inch-thick slices, *divided*

1 cup chicken broth

1 tsp. garlic powder

½ tsp. salt

¼ tsp. pepper

½ cup heavy cream

Nonstick cooking spray

¼ lb. bacon, cut in 1-inch squares, browned until crisp, and drained, *divided*

2 cups shredded cheddar cheese, *divided*

1. Place the potato slices, broth, garlic powder, salt, and pepper in the inner pot of the Instant Pot.

2. Secure the lid and set the vent to sealing. Manually set the cook time for 1 minute.

3. When the cook time is over, let the pressure release naturally for 3 minutes, then manually release the remaining pressure.

4. When the pin drops, remove the lid. Drain the potatoes, reserving the liquid. Set the potatoes aside for a moment, and return the liquid back to the inner pot.

5. Set the Instant Pot to the Sauté function. Stir in the heavy cream. Let the mixture simmer for a couple minutes.

6. Preheat the oven to 375°F.

7. Spray a 7-inch round baking dish or pie dish with nonstick cooking spray. Layer in half of the potatoes, half of the bacon, half of the cheese, and half of the cream sauce. Repeat this process with the remaining potatoes, bacon, cheese, and sauce.

8. Place the baking dish into the oven for 15 minutes, or until bubbly.

Vegetable Medley

Teena Wagner, Waterloo, ON

Makes 8 servings
Prep. Time: 20 minutes   ♨   Cook Time: 2 minutes

2 medium parsnips

4 medium carrots

1 turnip, about 4½ inches diameter

1 cup water

1 tsp. salt

3 Tbsp. turbinado sugar, or sugar of your choice

2 Tbsp. canola or olive oil

½ tsp. salt

1. Clean and peel the vegetables. Cut in ½-inch to 1-inch pieces.

2. Place the cup of water and 1 teaspoon of salt into the Instant Pot inner pot with the vegetables.

3. Secure the lid and make sure the vent is on sealing. Press Manual and set for 2 minutes.

4. When the cook time is over, release the pressure manually and press Cancel. Drain the water from the inner pot.

5. Press Sauté, add the veggies back into the inner pot and stir in the sugar, oil, and salt. Cook until the sugar is dissolved. Serve.

Squash Apple Bake

Lavina Hochstedler, Grand Blanc, MI

Makes 8 servings
Prep. Time: 10 minutes ⚹ *Cook Time: 5 minutes*

3 cups cubed butternut squash, *divided*

2½ Tbsp. honey, or brown sugar

¼ cup orange, or apple, juice

1½ tsp. cornstarch

2 apples, cut in short thick slices, *divided*

3 Tbsp. cup raisins, *divided*

¾ tsp. cinnamon

3 tsp. butter

1 cup water

1. Slice the butternut squash into ¾-inch rounds. Peel and cut into cubes.

2. Combine the honey, juice, and cornstarch in a small bowl.

3. In a greased 7-inch round baking dish, layer in half the squash, followed by a layer of half the apples, and then a layer of half the raisins.

4. Repeat layers.

5. Sprinkle with the cinnamon.

6. Pour the juice mixture over all.

7. Dot with butter.

8. Pour the water into the inner pot of the Instant Pot and place the trivet on top.

9. Place the baking dish on top of the trivet. Secure the lid and set the vent to sealing.

10. Manually set the cook time for 5 minutes on high pressure.

11. When the cook time is over, let the pressure release naturally for 15 minutes, then manually release the remaining pressure.

Baked Acorn Squash

Dale Peterson, Rapid City, SD

Makes 4 servings
Prep. Time: 25 minutes ♣ Cook Time: 5 minutes

2 small (1 ¼ lb. each) acorn squash
½ cup cracker crumbs
¼ cup coarsely chopped pecans
2 Tbsp. light, soft tub margarine, melted
3 Tbsp. brown sugar
¼ tsp. salt
¼ tsp. ground nutmeg
2 Tbsp. orange juice
1 cup water

1. Cut the squash in half. Remove the seeds.

2. Combine the remaining ingredients. Spoon this mixture into the squash halves.

3. Place the trivet inside the inner pot of the Instant Pot and pour in the water. Place the squash halves on top of the trivet.

4. Secure the lid and set the vent to sealing. Press Manual and set the time for 5 minutes.

5. When the cook time is over, let the pressure release naturally.

Sweet Potato Puree

Colleen Heatwole, Burton, MI

Makes 4–6 servings
Prep. Time: 10 minutes ⚜ Cook Time: 6 minutes

3 lb. sweet potatoes, peeled and cut into roughly 2-inch cubes

1 cup water

2 Tbsp. butter

1 tsp. salt

2 tsp. packed brown sugar

2 tsp. lemon juice

½ tsp. cinnamon

⅛ tsp. nutmeg, *optional*

1. Place the sweet potatoes and water in the inner pot of the Instant Pot.

2. Secure the lid, make sure the vent is on sealing, then cook for 6 minutes on high using the Manual setting.

3. Manually release the pressure when the cook time is over.

4. Drain the sweet potatoes and place them in a large mixing bowl. Mash with a potato masher or hand mixer.

5. Once thoroughly mashed, add remaining ingredients.

6. Taste and adjust seasonings to taste.

7. Serve immediately while still hot.

Decadent Sweet Potato "Casserole"

Hope Comerford, Clinton Township, MI

Makes 8–10 servings
Prep. Time: 10 minutes ❧ Cook Time: 8 minutes

4–5 medium sweet potatoes, peeled and chopped into ½-inch chunks

2 apples, peeled, cored, and chopped into ½-inch chunks

1 cup water

1 stick butter

1 tsp. vanilla extract

½ tsp. cinnamon

½ cup brown sugar

2 cups mini marshmallows

Tip:

You could use a kitchen torch to brown the marshmallows. Alternately, you could transfer the contents of the Instant Pot to a baking dish after Step 7, sprinkle with the marshmallows, and place under the broiler in the oven for a few minutes to brown/melt the marshmallows.

1. Place the sweet potato and apple chunks into the inner pot of the Instant Pot along with the water.

2. Secure the lid and set the vent to sealing. Manually set the cook time for 3 minutes.

3. When the cook time is over, manually release the pressure.

4. When the pin drops, remove the lid, then carefully remove the sweet potatoes and apples to a strainer and dispose of the liquid. Wipe out the inner pot.

5. Set the Instant Pot to the Sauté function. Add the butter and let it melt.

6. Stir in the vanilla, cinnamon, and brown sugar and cook until smooth and bubbly.

7. Add the sweet potatoes and apples back into the inner pot and stir to coat everything. Press Cancel.

8. Sprinkle the marshmallows over the top of the casserole. Cover the Instant Pot for a few minutes, until the marshmallows are melted, then serve.

Mashed Potatoes

Colleen Heatwole, Burton, MI

Makes 3–4 servings
Prep Time: 10 minutes & Cook Time: 5 minutes

1 cup water

6 medium potatoes, peeled and quartered

2 Tbsp. unsalted butter

½ to ¾ cup milk, warmed

Salt to taste

Pepper to taste

1. Add the water to the inner pot of the Instant Pot. Put the steamer basket in the pot and place the potatoes in the basket.

2. Seal the lid and make sure the vent is on sealing. Using Manual mode, select 5 minutes cook time, high pressure.

3. When cook time ends, do a manual release. Use a fork to test the potatoes. If needed, relock the lid and cook at high pressure a few minutes more.

4. Transfer the potatoes to a large mixing bowl. Mash using a hand mixer, stirring in the butter. Gradually add the warmed milk. Season with salt and pepper to taste.

Garlic Roasted Sweet Potatoes

Hope Comerford, Clinton Township, MI

Makes 4 servings
Prep. Time: 13 minutes ♣ Cook Time: 3 minutes

2 Tbsp. olive oil

2 sweet potatoes, peeled and cut into
1-inch chunks

1 small onion, cut into thick strips

6 large cloves garlic, minced

1½ cup vegetable broth

½ cup vegetable broth

1 tsp. fresh chopped thyme

1 tsp. sea salt

¼ tsp. pepper

1. Set the Instant Pot to the Sauté function and heat the oil.

2. Add the sweet potatoes and continue to sauté for about 10 minutes, or until browned on each side. Do this in batches if necessary.

3. Remove the potatoes and set aside.

4. Add the onion and garlic to the inner pot of the Instant Pot and sauté for 3 minutes.

5. Pour in the vegetable broth and scrape the bottom of the inner pot with a wooden spoon or spatula. Press Cancel.

6. Add the sweet potatoes back in, and season with the chopped thyme, salt, and pepper.

7. Secure the lid and set the vent to sealing. Manually set the cook time for 3 minutes on high pressure.

8. When the cook time is over, manually release the pressure.

9. When the pin drops, remove the lid. With a slotted spoon, remove the potatoes from the pot and serve.

Potato Bacon Gratin

Valerie Drobel, Carlisle, PA

Makes 8 servings
Prep. Time: 20 minutes   ♣   Cook Time: 40 minutes

1 Tbsp. olive oil

6-oz. bag fresh spinach

1 clove garlic, minced

4 large potatoes, peeled or unpeeled, *divided*

6 oz. Canadian bacon slices, *divided*

5 oz. reduced-fat grated Swiss cheese, *divided*

1 cup lower-sodium, lower-fat chicken broth

1. Set the Instant Pot to Sauté and pour in the olive oil. Cook the spinach and garlic in olive oil just until spinach is wilted (5 minutes or less). Turn off the Instant Pot.

2. Cut the potatoes into thin slices, about ¼-inch thick.

3. Spray a springform pan that will fit into the inner pot of the Instant Pot with nonstick cooking spray, then layer ⅓ the potatoes, half the bacon, ⅓ the cheese, and half the wilted spinach.

4. Repeat layers ending with potatoes. Reserve ⅓ cheese for later.

5. Pour the chicken broth over all.

6. Wipe the bottom of the Instant Pot to soak up any remaining oil, then add 2 cups of water and the steaming rack. Place the springform pan on top.

7. Close the lid and secure to the locking position. Be sure the vent is turned to sealing. Set for 35 minutes on Manual at high pressure.

8. Perform a quick release.

9. Top with the remaining cheese, then allow to stand 10 minutes before removing from the Instant Pot, cutting, and serving.

Cheesy Potatoes

Hope Comerford, Clinton Township, MI

Makes 8 servings
Prep. Time: 5 minutes ⚘ *Cook Time: 3 minutes*

2 Tbsp. butter

1 cup chopped onion

2 cloves garlic, chopped

1 cup chicken broth

30-oz. pkg. frozen hash browns, diced or shredded

1 cup sour cream

1 tsp. sea salt

1 tsp. onion powder

1 tsp. garlic powder

¼ tsp. pepper

2 cups shredded cheddar cheese

1 cup panko bread crumbs, *optional*

1. Set the Instant Pot to the Sauté function. Add the butter to the inner pot and let it melt.

2. Sauté the onion and garlic in the butter for 3 minutes.

3. Pour in the chicken broth and scrape the bottom of the inner pot with a wooden spoon or spatula. Press Cancel.

4. Place the steamer basket into the inner pot and pour the frozen hash browns into that.

5. Secure the lid and set the vent to sealing. Manually set the cook time for 3 minutes.

6. When the cook time is over, manually release the pressure.

7. When the pin drops, remove the lid, carefully pour the hash browns from the steamer basket into the inner pot, and stir in the sour cream, sea salt, onion powder, garlic powder, pepper and shredded cheese.

8. If you choose, you can transfer the contents of the inner pot to an oven-safe baking dish. You would then top the potatoes with the bread crumbs and put them under the broiler for 2 to 3 minutes.

Cheesy Broccoli Rice Casserole

Hope Comerford, Clinton Township, MI

Makes 4 servings
Prep. Time: 10 minutes ♠ Cook Time: 6 minutes

1 Tbsp. olive oil

¾ cup chopped onion

4 oz. fresh sliced mushrooms

2 cups rice

1 tsp. garlic powder

1 tsp. salt

¼ tsp. pepper

2½ cups chicken broth, *divided*

2 cups chopped broccoli florets

1½ cups shredded cheddar cheese

1. Set the Instant Pot to Sauté mode and heat the oil.

2. Sauté the onion and mushrooms in the oil for about 3 minutes. Press Cancel.

3. Add the rice, garlic powder, salt, pepper, and 2 cups of the broth. Stir.

4. Secure the lid and set the vent to sealing. Manually set the cook time for 5 minutes on high pressure.

5. When the cook time is over, manually release the pressure. When the pin drops, remove the lid.

6. Stir in the broccoli and remaining ½ cup of broth.

7. Secure the lid and set the vent to sealing. Manually set the cook time for 1 minute on high pressure.

8. When the cook time is over, manually release the pressure.

9. When the pin drops, remove the lid and stir in the cheese.

Bacon Ranch Red Potatoes

Hope Comerford, Clinton Township, MI

Makes 6 servings
Prep. Time: 15 minutes ❧ Cook Time: 7 minutes

4 strips bacon, chopped into small pieces

2 lb. red potatoes, diced

1 Tbsp. fresh chopped parsley

1 tsp. sea salt

4 cloves garlic, chopped

1-oz. packet ranch dressing/seasoning mix

⅓ cup water

½ cup shredded sharp white cheddar

2 Tbsp. chopped scallions for garnish

1. Set the Instant Pot to Sauté, add the bacon to the inner pot, and cook until crisp.

2. Stir in the potatoes, parsley, sea salt, garlic, ranch dressing mix, and water.

3. Secure the lid, make sure the vent is on sealing, then set the Instant Pot to Manual for 7 minutes at high pressure.

4. When cooking time is up, do a quick release and carefully open the lid.

5. Stir in the cheese. Garnish with the scallions.

Hometown Spanish Rice

Beverly Flatt-Getz, Warriors Mark, PA

Makes 6–8 servings
Prep. Time: 8 minutes ☙ Cook Time: 3 minutes

1 Tbsp. olive oil

1 large onion, chopped

1 bell pepper, chopped

2 cups long-grain rice, rinsed

1½ cups low-sodium chicken stock

28-oz. can low-sodium stewed tomatoes with juice

Grated Parmesan cheese, *optional*

1. Set the Instant Pot to Sauté and heat the oil in the inner pot.

2. Sauté the onion and bell pepper in the inner pot for about 3 to 5 minutes.

3. Add the rice and continue to sauté for about 1 more minute. Press Cancel.

4. Add the chicken stock and stewed tomatoes into the inner pot, in that order.

5. Secure the lid and set the vent to sealing.

6. Manually set the cook time for 3 minutes on high pressure.

7. When the cook time is over, let the pressure release naturally for 10 minutes, then manually release the remaining pressure.

8. When the pin drops, remove the lid. Fluff the rice with a fork.

9. Sprinkle with Parmesan cheese just before serving, if you wish.

Apple-Cranberry Wild Rice

Heather Horst, Lebanon, PA

Makes 6 cups
Prep. Time: 5 minutes & Cook Time: 20 minutes

½ cup raw brown rice

½ cup raw wild rice

I tsp. dried savory

I small leek (white portion only), coarsely chopped, or 3 Tbsp. chopped onion

I tsp. olive oil

⅓ cup dried cranberries

¼ cup chopped dried apples

½ tsp. onion powder

½ tsp. lemon-pepper seasoning

I ½ cups low-sodium vegetable stock

I cup water

1. Place the ingredients into the inner pot in the order shown. Secure the lid and set the vent to sealing.

2. Manually set the cook time for 20 minutes on high pressure.

3. When the cook time is over, let the pressure release naturally.

Perfect Pinto Beans

Hope Comerford, Clinton Township, MI

Makes 8 servings
Prep. Time: 2 minutes ⚬ *Cook Time: 50 minutes*

1 large onion, chopped

1 lb. dry pinto beans, sorted and rinsed

6 cups vegetable or chicken broth

2 bay leaves

1½ tsp. sea salt

1 tsp. cumin

½ tsp. paprika

¼ tsp. pepper

1. Place all ingredients into the inner pot of the Instant Pot.

2. Secure the lid and set the vent to sealing. Manually set the cook time for 50 minutes on high pressure.

3. When the cook time is over, let the pressure release naturally for 15 minutes, then manually release the remaining pressure.

Baked Beans

Hope Comerford, Clinton Township, MI

Makes 20 or more servings
Prep. Time: 10 minutes ⚶ Cook Time: 60 minutes

16 oz. navy beans, rinsed

9½ cups water, *divided*

12 oz. salt pork, chopped into small strips

1 large onion, chopped

1 cup ketchup

¾ cup dark brown sugar

3 Tbsp. mustard

NOTE:

These will thicken as they cool.

1. Place the navy beans and 9 cups of water in the inner pot of the Instant Pot.

2. Secure the lid and set the vent to sealing. Manually set the cook time for 15 minutes on high pressure.

3. When the cook time is over, let the pressure release naturally for 20 minutes, then manually release the remaining pressure.

4. When the pin drops, remove the lid. Drain and rinse the beans. Rinse out the inner pot and wipe it dry.

5. Set the Instant Pot to the Sauté function. Let it get very hot, then add the salt pork. Sauté for a few minutes, and when the fat really starts to render, add the onion and continue to sauté for a couple more minutes.

6. Pour in ½ cup of water and scrape up any bits from the bottom with a wooden spatula or spoon. Press Cancel.

7. Mix the ketchup, brown sugar, and mustard.

8. Pour the remaining water into the inner pot. Add half the beans, then half of the ketchup sauce. Finish with the remaining beans and ketchup sauce.

9. Secure the lid and set the vent to sealing. Manually set the cook time for 35 minutes.

10. When the cook time is over, let the pressure release naturally for 20 minutes, then manually release the remaining pressure.

11. When the pin drops, remove the lid and stir the beans. Press Cancel.

Calico Beans

Hope Comerford, Clinton Township, MI

Makes 8 servings
Prep. Time: 12 minutes ⚬ Cook Time: 15 minutes

Nonstick cooking spray

6 slices bacon, diced

1 cup chopped red onion

3 cloves garlic, chopped

1 lb. lean ground beef

¾ cups vegetable or chicken broth

15-oz. can pork and beans

15-oz. can kidney beans, drained

15-oz. can lima beans, drained

¾ cup ketchup

½ cup brown sugar

2 tsp. mustard

1½ Tbsp. apple cider vinegar

1 tsp. sea salt

¼ tsp. pepper

1. Set the Instant Pot to the Sauté function and let it get nice and hot. Spray the inner pot with nonstick cooking spray and then add the bacon. Sauté until crispy.

2. Add the onion and garlic and sauté for an additional 1 minute.

3. Add the ground beef and cook until browned and crumbly.

4. Pour in the broth and scrape the bottom of the pot with a wooden spoon or spatula to bring up any stuck-on bits. Press Cancel.

5. Add the remaining ingredients and stir.

6. Secure the lid and set the vent to sealing. Manually set the cook time for 15 minutes on high pressure.

7. When the cook time is over, let the pressure release naturally for 5 minutes, then manually release the remaining pressure.

Black-Eyed Peas and Greens

Hope Comerford, Clinton Township, MI

Makes 6 servings
Prep. Time: 8 minutes   Cook Time: 15 minutes

Nonstick cooking spray

4–5 slices of thick-cut bacon, chopped

1 cup chopped onion

4 cloves garlic, chopped

1 lb. collard greens, washed, stems trimmed, chopped

1 lb. dry black-eyed peas, sorted and rinsed

4 cups chicken broth

2 cups water

1 tsp. sea salt

¼ tsp. pepper

1. Set the Instant Pot to the Sauté function and let it get nice and hot. Spray the inner pot with nonstick cooking spray and then add the bacon. Sauté until crispy.

2. Add the onion and garlic and sauté for an additional 1 minute.

3. Add the collard greens and stir until wilted. Press Cancel.

4. Stir in the remaining ingredients.

5. Secure the lid and set the vent to sealing. Manually set the cook time for 15 minutes on high pressure.

6. When the cook time is over, let the pressure release naturally.

7. When the pin drops, remove the lid and stir. If it needs to thicken, you can switch the Instant Pot over to Sauté mode and let it simmer for another 15 minutes or so.

Stuffing Ring

Hope Comerford, Clinton Township, MI

Makes 4–6 servings
Prep. Time: 10 minutes ⚓ Cook Time: 20–30 minutes

4 Tbsp. butter

1 cup chopped celery

1 cup chopped onion

½ lb. extra-lean ground beef

1 tsp. sea salt

1 tsp. garlic powder

1 tsp. onion powder

1 tsp. poultry seasoning

½ tsp. sage

¼ tsp. pepper

8 oz. stuffing cubes (seasoned or unseasoned)

1¼ cups chicken or turkey stock

1½ cups water

Variation:

You can keep this meatless by omitting the ground beef and using vegetarian stock.

1. Set the Instant Pot to the Sauté function and melt the butter.

2. Sauté the celery and onion for about 3 minutes, then add the ground beef and all of the seasonings, browning it. When the beef is browned, press Cancel.

3. Remove the beef mixture from the inner pot into a large bowl and mix with the stuffing cubes and stock. Wipe out the pot.

4. Pour in the water and place the trivet on top with handles up.

5. Spray a 7-inch Bundt pan with nonstick cooking spray. Spoon the stuffing mixture into the Bundt pan, pressing down. You'll be surprised how much you can pack in there!

6. Cover the pan with foil and place on top of the trivet.

7. Secure the lid and set the vent to sealing. Manually set the cook time for 15 minutes on high pressure.

8. When the cook time is over, manually release the pressure.

9. When the pin drops, remove the lid, then carefully remove the trivet with hot pads. Set the stuffing on a cooling rack.

10. You can serve this as is, by unmolding it from the ring on a serving platter, or you can unmold it onto a baking pan lined with silicone or greased foil and place it in a 350°F oven for 5 to 10 minutes to brown up the outside.

Sour Cream Corn Bread

Edwina Stoltzfus, Narvon, PA

Makes 9 servings
Prep. Time: 10 minutes & Cook Time: 55 minutes

Egg substitute equivalent to 1 egg, or 2 egg whites, beaten

¼ cup skim milk

2 Tbsp. canola oil

1 cup fat-free sour cream

¾ cup cornmeal

½ cup whole wheat flour

½ cup all-purpose flour

¼ cup turbinado sugar, or sugar of your choice

2 tsp. baking powder

½ tsp. baking soda

Nonstick cooking spray

1 cup water

1. Place the egg substitute in a large mixing bowl and beat.

2. Add the milk, oil, and sour cream and combine well.

3. In a separate bowl, combine all dry ingredients.

4. Add the dry ingredients to the wet ones. Mix together just until moistened.

5. Spoon into a 7x3-inch round baking pan sprayed lightly with nonstick cooking spray. Wrap the top tightly with foil, then take a second piece of foil and wrap the bottom too.

6. Pour the water into the inner pot of the Instant Pot. Place the trivet on top.

7. Place the foil-wrapped baking pan on the trivet. Secure the lid and set the vent to sealing.

8. Manually set the time to cook for 55 minutes on high pressure.

9. When the cook time is over, let the pressure release naturally for 10 minutes, then manually release the remaining pressure.

10. Carefully remove the trivet with oven mitts. Wipe any moisture off of the foil, then carefully remove the foil from the pan.

11. Serve warm!

Desserts

Christmas Cheesecake

Hope Comerford, Clinton Township, MI

Makes 6 servings
Prep. Time: 15 minutes   ⚜   Cook Time: 35 minutes

Nonstick cooking spray

Crust:

12 whole gluten-free chocolate sandwich cookies, crushed into crumbs

2 Tbsp. salted butter, melted

Cheesecake:

16 oz. cream cheese, room temperature

½ cup granulated sugar

2 large eggs, room temperature

1 Tbsp. gluten-free all-purpose flour

¼ cup heavy cream

1 tsp. pure vanilla extract

1 tsp. peppermint extract

¼ cup crushed peppermint candy

1½ cups water

Topping:

¼ cup crushed peppermint candies

¼ cup chocolate sauce

1. Tightly wrap the bottom of a 7-inch springform pan in foil. Spray the inside with nonstick cooking spray.

2. In a small bowl, stir together the crushed gluten-free chocolate sandwich cookies and melted butter. Press the crumbs into the bottom of the prepared pan. (I find the bottom of a glass cup is a great tool to use for this.) Place this in the freezer for 10–15 minutes.

3. In a large bowl, beat the cream cheese until smooth. (You can use an electric mixer or stand mixer with paddle attachment.)

4. Add the sugar and mix until combined.

5. Add the eggs, one at a time, making sure each is fully incorporated before adding the next. Be sure to scrape down the bowl in between each egg.

6. Add the flour, heavy cream, vanilla, and peppermint extract, and continue to mix until smooth.

7. Gently fold in the crushed peppermint candy and pour this batter into the pan you had in the freezer.

8. Cover the top of the pan with a piece of foil.

9. Pour 1½ cups of water into the inner pot and place the trivet in the bottom of the pot.

10. Create a foil sling by folding a 20-inch-long piece of foil in half lengthwise two times. This sling will allow you to easily place and remove the springform pan from the pot.

(Continued on next page)

11. Place the cheesecake pan in the center of the sling and carefully lower the pan into the inner pot. Fold down the excess foil from the sling to ensure the pot closes properly.

12. Lock the lid into place and make sure the vent is on sealing. Press the Manual button and cook on high pressure for 35 minutes.

13. When the Instant Pot beeps, hit the Keep Warm/Cancel button to turn off the pressure cooker. Allow the pressure to release naturally for 10 minutes and then do a quick release to release any pressure remaining in the pot.

14. Carefully remove the lid. Gently unfold the foil sling and remove the cheesecake from the pot to a cooling rack using the foil sling handles. Uncover the cheesecake and allow it to cool to room temperature.

15. Once the cheesecake has cooled, refrigerate it for at least 8 hours, or overnight.

16. Before serving, top with ¼ cup peppermint candies and drizzle the chocolate sauce over the top.

Tip:

You do not have to use gluten-free cookies. You may make this with regular cookies.

German Chocolate Bundt Cake with Coconut Pecan Frosting

Hope Comerford, Clinton Township, MI

Makes 8 servings

Prep. Time: 35 minutes ⚘ *Cook Time: 30 minutes* ⚘ *Cooling Time: 60 minutes*

Batter:

1½ cups all-purpose flour

½ cup sugar

2½ Tbsp. unsweetened cocoa powder

1¼ tsp. baking soda

½ tsp. salt

⅓ cup vegetable oil

1 Tbsp. white vinegar

½ tsp. vanilla extract

2½ cups water, *divided*

Frosting:

1 cup evaporated milk

3 egg yolks

½ cup butter

1 cup white sugar

1¼ tsp. vanilla extract

1¼ cups sweetened coconut flakes

¾ cups chopped pecans

1. In a medium bowl, mix together the flour, sugar, cocoa powder, baking soda, and salt.

2. In a small bowl, mix together the vegetable oil, vinegar, vanilla, and 1 cup of water.

3. Pour the contents of the small bowl into the medium bowl of dry ingredients and combine until the batter is smooth.

4. Pour the batter into a greased 7-inch Bundt cake pan. Cover with aluminum foil.

5. Pour the remaining 1½ cups of water into the inner pot of the Instant Pot and place a trivet (or silicone sling) with handles on top of the water. Carefully lower the Bundt cake pan on top of the trivet.

6. Secure the lid and set the vent to sealing. Manually set the cook time for 30 minutes on high pressure.

7. Meanwhile, begin the frosting. In a medium saucepan, whisk together the milk and egg yolks over medium heat. Stir in the butter and sugar.

8. Set a timer for 20 minutes, continuing to cook and whisk the contents of the saucepan over medium heat.

9. Remove the saucepan from the heat and stir in the vanilla, coconut flakes, and pecans. Once combined, let the frosting cool and thicken.

(Continued on page 165)

10. When the cook time is over on the Instant Pot, manually release the pressure.

11. Carefully remove the Bundt pan and place on a cooling rack for about 10 minutes, then release the cake from the pan to cool for about another 50 minutes.

12. When the cake is completely cooled, frost it with the coconut pecan frosting. Serve and enjoy!

Creamy Orange Cheesecake

Jeanette Oberholtzer, Manheim, PA

Makes 10 servings
Prep. Time: 35 minutes & Cook Time: 35 minutes
Cooling Time: 2 or more hours & Chilling Time: 8 hours

Crust:

¾ cup graham cracker crumbs

2 Tbsp. sugar

3 Tbsp. melted, soft tub margarine

Filling:

2 (8-oz.) packages cream cheese, at room temperature

⅔ cup sugar

2 eggs

I egg yolk

¼ cup frozen orange juice concentrate

I tsp. orange zest

I Tbsp. flour

½ tsp. vanilla extract

I½ cups water

1. Combine crust ingredients. Pat into 7-inch springform pan.

2. Cream together the cream cheese and sugar. Add the eggs and yolk. Beat for 3 minutes.

3. Beat in the juice, zest, flour, and vanilla. Beat 2 minutes.

4. Pour the batter into the crust. Cover with foil.

5. Place the trivet into the Instant Pot and pour in the water. Place a foil sling on top of the trivet, then place the springform pan on top.

6. Secure the lid and make sure lid is set to sealing. Press Manual and set for 35 minutes.

7. When the cook time is over, press Cancel and allow the pressure to release naturally for 7 minutes, then release the remaining pressure manually.

8. Carefully remove the springform pan by using hot pads to lift the pan up by the foil sling. Uncover and place on a cooling rack until cool, then refrigerate for 8 hours.

Dump Cake

Janice Muller, Derwood, MD

Makes 15 servings
Prep. Time: 20 minutes ☙ Cook Time: 50 minutes

Nonstick cooking spray

20-oz. can crushed pineapple

21-oz. can blueberry or cherry pie filling

18½-oz. package yellow cake mix

Cinnamon

⅓ cup light, soft tub margarine

⅓ cup chopped walnuts

1 cup water

1. Grease the bottom and sides of a 7-inch springform pan.

2. Spread layers of pineapple, blueberry pie filling, and dry cake mix. Be careful not to mix the layers.

3. Sprinkle with cinnamon.

4. Top with thin layers of margarine chunks and nuts.

5. Cover the pan with foil.

6. Place the trivet into the Instant Pot and pour in the water. Place a foil sling on top of the trivet, then place the springform pan on top.

7. Secure the lid and make sure lid is set to sealing. Press Steam and set for 50 minutes.

8. When the cook time is over, release the pressure manually, then carefully remove the springform pan by using hot pads to lift the pan up by the foil sling. Place on a cooling rack until cool.

Variation:

Use a package of spice cake mix and apple pie filling.

Cherry Delight

Anna Musser, Manheim, PA
Marianne J. Troyer, Millersburg, OH

Makes 12 servings
Prep. Time: 20 minutes ⚜ Cook Time: 50 minutes

Nonstick cooking spray
20-oz. can cherry pie filling, light
½ package yellow cake mix
¼ cup soft tub margarine, melted
⅓ cup walnuts, *optional*
I cup water

1. Grease a 7-inch springform pan then pour the pie filling inside.

2. Combine the dry cake mix and the margarine (mixture will be crumbly) in a bowl. Sprinkle over filling. Sprinkle with walnuts.

3. Cover the pan with foil.

4. Place the trivet into the Instant Pot and pour in the water. Place a foil sling on top of the trivet, then place the springform pan on top.

5. Secure the lid and make sure lid is set to sealing. Press Steam and set for 50 minutes.

6. When the cook time is over, release the pressure manually, then carefully remove the springform pan by using hot pads to lift the pan up by the foil sling. Place on a cooling rack for 1–2 hours.

Serving suggestion:
Serve in bowls with scoops of ice cream.

Carrot Cake

Colleen Heatwole, Burton, MI

Makes 10 servings
Prep. Time: 35 minutes & Cook Time: 50 minutes

⅓ cup canola oil

2 eggs

1 Tbsp. hot water

½ cup grated raw carrots

¾ cup flour and 2 Tbsp. flour, *divided*

¾ cup sugar

½ tsp. baking powder

⅛ tsp. salt

¼ tsp. ground allspice

½ tsp. ground cinnamon

⅛ tsp. ground cloves

½ cup chopped nuts

½ cup raisins or chopped dates

1 cup water

1. In a large bowl, beat the oil, eggs, and water for 1 minute.

2. Add the carrots. Mix well.

3. Stir together the flour, sugar, baking powder, salt, allspice, cinnamon, and cloves. Add to the creamed mixture.

4. Toss the nuts and raisins in a bowl with 2 tablespoons of flour. Add to creamed mixture. Mix well.

5. Pour into greased and floured 7-inch springform pan and cover with foil.

6. Place the trivet into the Instant Pot and pour in the water. Place a foil sling on top of the trivet, then place the springform pan on top.

7. Secure the lid and make sure lid is set to sealing. Press Steam and set for 50 minutes.

8. When the cook time is over, release the pressure manually, then carefully remove the springform pan by using hot pads to lift the pan up by the foil sling. Place on a cooling rack until cool.

Lemon Pudding Cake

Jean Butzer, Batavia, NY

Makes 6 servings
Prep. Time: 15 minutes ⚬ Cook Time: 40 minutes

3 eggs, separated

I tsp. grated lemon peel

¼ cup lemon juice

I Tbsp. melted soft tub margarine

I ½ cups fat-free half-and-half

½ cup sugar plus 2 Tbsp. sugar

¼ cup flour

⅛ tsp. salt

I cup water

1. Beat the egg whites until stiff peaks form. Set aside.

2. Beat the egg yolks. Blend in the lemon peel, lemon juice, margarine, and half-and-half.

3. In separate bowl, combine the sugar, flour, and salt. Add to egg-lemon mixture, beating until smooth.

4. Fold into beaten egg whites.

5. Spoon into a greased and floured 7-inch springform pan. Cover with foil.

6. Place the trivet into the Instant Pot with the water. Place a foil sling on top of the trivet, then place the springform pan on top of the trivet.

7. Secure the lid and make sure lid is set to sealing. Press Manual and set time for 40 minutes.

8. Perform a quick release of the pressure when cooking time is done. Remove the springform pan carefully using hot pads with the foil sling and let cool on a cooling rack.

Pumpkin Pie

Hope Comerford, Clinton Township, MI

Makes 10 servings
Prep. Time: 20 minutes 🌿 Cook Time: 30 minutes 🌿 Cooling Time: 60 minutes

Graham Cracker Crust:
1¼ cups graham cracker crumbs
6 Tbsp. butter, melted
¼ cup white sugar
Nonstick cooking spray

Filling:
15-oz. can pumpkin puree
14-oz. can sweetened condensed milk
2 medium eggs
1½ tsp. pumpkin pie spice
¼ tsp. salt
1 cup water

1. In a food processor, mix the graham cracker crumbs, butter, and sugar. If you don't have a food processor, mix them in a bowl.

2. Spray a 7-inch springform pan with nonstick baking spray. Pour the crust mixture into the pan and press the mixture into the bottom and around the sides of the pan. I like to use the bottom of a glass, but you can use your fingers or a spatula. Place this in the freezer for 15 minutes.

3. In a medium bowl, mix the filling ingredients until they are smooth.

4. When the crust comes out of the freezer, pour in the filling.

5. Pour the cup of water into the bottom of the inner pot of the Instant Pot. Lower the trivet into the pot with the handles up. Carefully place the pumpkin pie pan on top.

6. Secure the lid and set the vent to sealing. Manually set the cook time for 30 minutes on high pressure.

7. When the cook time is over, let the pressure release naturally for 10 minutes, then manually release the remaining pressure.

8. Carefully remove the pie using the handles of the trivet (use heat resistant gloves). Set on a cooling rack for 1 hour. If not eating right away, place in the refrigerator.

Rice Pudding

Janie Steele, Moore, OK

Makes 6–8 servings
Prep. Time: 5 minutes & Cook Time: 14 minutes

1½ Tbsp. butter
1 cup uncooked rice
½ cup sugar
1 cup water
2 cups milk (2% works best)
1 egg
¼ cup evaporated milk
½ tsp vanilla extract
½ tsp. almond extract, *optional*
Nutmeg, *optional*
Cinnamon, *optional*

1. In the inner pot of the Instant Pot, sauté the butter until melted using the Sauté setting. Add the rice, sugar, water, and milk, then stir.

2. Secure the lid and make sure the vent is set to sealing. Manually set the cook time for 14 minutes on high pressure. Let the pressure release naturally when the cook time is over.

3. In a bowl, whisk together the egg and evaporated milk.

4. Add a spoonful of the rice mixture to the egg and milk mixture and stir.

5. Return all to the inner pot and stir in the vanilla and optional almond extract.

6. Use the Sauté function and bring mixture to bubble for 30 to 60 seconds.

7. Stir slowly so it does not stick to the pot.

8. Use nutmeg or cinnamon to garnish if desired.

Instant Pot Tapioca

Nancy W. Huber, Green Park, PA

Makes 6 servings
Prep. Time: 10 minutes ☙ Cook Time: 7 minutes ☙ Chilling Time: 4 hours

2 cups water
I cup small pearl tapioca
4 eggs
½ cup evaporated skim milk
¾ cup sugar
I tsp. vanilla extract
Fruit of choice, *optional*

1. Combine the water and tapioca in the inner pot of the Instant Pot.

2. Secure the lid and make sure the vent is on sealing. Press Manual and set for 5 minutes.

3. Perform a quick release. Press Cancel, remove the lid, and press Sauté.

4. Whisk together the eggs and evaporated milk. Slowly add this mixture to the Instant Pot, stirring constantly so the eggs don't scramble.

5. Stir in the sugar until it's dissolved, press Cancel, then stir in the vanilla.

6. Allow to cool thoroughly, then refrigerate for at least 4 hours.

7. Serve with fruit of your choice if desired.

Caramel Corn

Hope Comerford, Clinton Township, MI

Makes 5–6 servings
Prep. Time: 3 minutes   Cook Time: 15 minutes

2 Tbsp. coconut oil

½ cup popcorn kernels

½ tsp. sea salt

Caramel Sauce:

½ cup sweet cream salted butter

½ cup light brown sugar

2 Tbsp. heavy cream

1 tsp. vanilla extract

¼ tsp. baking soda

1. Set the Instant Pot to the Sauté function. Add the coconut oil and let it melt.

2. When the oil is melted, add the popcorn kernels, stir, then secure the lid. Let it cook for about 3 minutes, or until you do not hear kernels popping.

3. Press "cancel" and move the popcorn to a bowl. Toss with the salt.

4. Place the inner pot back into the Instant Pot base and press the Sauté function.

5. Add the butter and let it melt. Once it's melted, add the brown sugar and heavy cream. When the sugar is dissolved add the vanilla and baking soda. Continue to cook until the sauce has thickened into caramel.

6. Press cancel on the Instant Pot. Add the popcorn back into the inner pot and gently stir to coat it with the caramel sauce.

7. Line a baking sheet with parchment paper, foil, or a silicone mat. Pour the caramel corn onto the baking sheet in a single layer and let it cool.

Metric Equivalent Measurements

If you're accustomed to using metric measurements, I don't want you to be inconvenienced by the imperial measurements I use in this book.

Use this handy chart, too, to figure out the size of the slow cooker you'll need for each recipe.

Weight (Dry Ingredients)

1 oz		30 g
4 oz	¼ lb	120 g
8 oz	½ lb	240 g
12 oz	¾ lb	360 g
16 oz	1 lb	480 g
32 oz	2 lb	960 g

Slow-Cooker Sizes

1-quart	0.96 l
2-quart	1.92 l
3-quart	2.88 l
4-quart	3.84 l
5-quart	4.80 l
6-quart	5.76 l
7-quart	6.72 l
8-quart	7.68 l

Volume (Liquid Ingredients)

½ tsp.		2 ml
1 tsp.		5 ml
1 Tbsp.	½ fl oz	15 ml
2 Tbsp.	1 fl oz	30 ml
¼ cup	2 fl oz	60 ml
⅓ cup	3 fl oz	80 ml
½ cup	4 fl oz	120 ml
⅔ cup	5 fl oz	160 ml
¾ cup	6 fl oz	180 ml
1 cup	8 fl oz	240 ml
1 pt	16 fl oz	480 ml
1 qt	32 fl oz	960 ml

Length

¼ in	6 mm
½ in	13 mm
¾ in	19 mm
1 in	25 mm
6 in	15 cm
12 in	30 cm

Recipe & Ingredient Index

White Chicken Chili, 45
wine
  red
    Instant Pot Boneless
      Short Ribs, 100
    Prime Rib, 87–88
  white
    Chicken Alfredo, 63
    Pumpkin Risotto, 117
Worcestershire sauce
  Barbecued Brisket, 95
  Beef Goulash, 105

Cottage Pie, 109–110
French Onion Soup, 43
Green Bean Casserole,
  125
Instantly Good Beef Stew,
  53
Sloppy Joes, 111

Y

yogurt
  Apple Cranberry Muffin
    Bites, 15

Z

zucchini
  Garden Vegetable
    Crustless Quiche, 17
  Turkey Peasant Soup, 26

About the Author

Hope Comerford is a mom, wife, elementary music teacher, blogger, recipe developer, public speaker, Young Living Essential Oils essential oil enthusiast/educator, and published author. In 2013, she was diagnosed with a severe gluten intolerance and since then has spent many hours creating easy, practical, and delicious gluten-free recipes that can be enjoyed by both those who are affected by gluten and those who are not.

Growing up, Hope spent many hours in the kitchen with her Meme (grandmother) and her love for cooking grew from there. While working on her master's degree when her daughter was young, Hope turned to her slow cookers for some salvation and sanity. It was from there she began truly experimenting with recipes and quickly learned she had the ability to get a little more creative in the kitchen and develop her own recipes.

In 2010, Hope started her blog, *A Busy Mom's Slow Cooker Adventures*, to simply share the recipes she was making with her family and friends. She never imagined people all over the world would begin visiting her page and sharing her recipes with others as well. In 2013, Hope self-published her first cookbook, *Slow Cooker Recipes 10 Ingredients or Less and Gluten-Free*, and then later wrote *The Gluten-Free Slow Cooker*.

Hope became the new brand ambassador and author of Fix-It and Forget-It in mid-2016. Since then, she has brought her excitement and creativeness to the Fix-It and Forget-It brand. Through Fix-It and Forget-It, she has written *Fix-It and Forget-It Healthy Slow Cooker Cookbook*, *Fix-It and Forget-It Healthy 5-Ingredient Cookbook*, *Fix-It and Forget-It Instant Pot Cookbook*, *Fix-It and Forget-It Plant-Based Comfort Foods Cookbook*, *Welcome Home Harvest Cookbook*, *Welcome Home Pies, Crisps and Crumbles*, *Fix-It and Forget-It Instant Pot Light & Healthy Cookbook*, and many more.

Hope lives in the city of Clinton Township, Michigan, near Metro Detroit. She has been happily married to her husband and best friend, Justin, since 2008. Together they have two children, Ella and Gavin, who are her motivation, inspiration, and heart. In her spare time, Hope enjoys traveling, singing, cooking, reading books, working on wooden puzzles, spending time with friends and family, and relaxing.